Johanna
Turner

Cognitive
Development
and
Education

Methuen

London and New York

To Sue and Roger

*First published in 1984 by
Methuen & Co. Ltd
11 New Fetter Lane, London EC4P 4EE*

*Published in the USA by
Methuen & Co.
in association with Methuen, Inc.
733 Third Avenue, New York, NY 10017*

© *1984 Johanna Turner*

*Typeset by Rowland Phototypesetting Ltd
Printed in Great Britain by
Richard Clay (The Chaucer Press) Ltd
Bungay, Suffolk*

British Library
Cataloguing in Publication Data

Turner, Johanna
Cognitive development and education.—
(New essential psychology)
1. Cognition in children
I. Title   II. Series
155.4'13   BF723.C5
ISBN 0-416-33670-1

Library of Congress
Cataloging in Publication Data

Turner, Johanna.
Cognitive development and education.

(New essential psychology)
Bibliography: p.
Includes index.
1. Learning, Psychology of. 2. Cognition in
children. 3. Child psychology. I. Title.
II. Series.
LB1051.T82   1984   370.15'2
83-17355
ISBN 0-416-33670-1

Contents

Acknowledgements

I would like to thank Mr Roger Goodwin, for suggesting material for the sections on language and memory; Mr Nicholas Tucker and Mr John Sants, discussions with whom refined my ideas and stimulated new areas of thought; and all my friends and colleagues in the School of Cultural and Community Studies at the University of Sussex. I would particularly like to thank Mrs Peggy Paine for typing and retyping the manuscript with rapidity, accuracy and patience.

The publishers and I would also like to thank the following for permission to use copyright material: Lawrence Erlbaum Associates for tables 1, 2 and 3; Methuen for figure 1; Wiley & Sons for figure 2.

1

Introduction

Approaches to cognitive development

Imagine a student sitting with this book before her (or, of course, him). As she glances around she will see objects and people. She will be able to categorize these objects as 'a chair', 'a table', and so on. She may notice, momentarily, a fly settling on the book or a bird flying past the window. She will be able to remember what has happened in the immediate or distant past and make plans for the future. She can communicate with people in the room, and abstract meanings from the symbols on this page. She may look at a picture on the wall or listen to a piece of music. Such behaviour is taken for granted, much is automatic, yet for it to happen at all requires the utilization of complex cognitive processes. Were she to become ill, or injured, had she been born blind, deaf, or brain-damaged, much behaviour that is now simple and obvious could become difficult, if not impossible. What, then, must she be doing in order to carry out such behaviours? First, she must be 'perceiving', 'attending to', 'taking in' the visual and auditory stimuli surrounding her. Secondly, she must be 'holding' these in her 'mind' while she decides what they are and whether to ignore the perception, for example, the momentary recognition of the fly, or store it for future use so as to remember what has happened or what she has read. The fact that she can recognize a 'chair' as a chair means that she is using previously stored memories and has developed both a concept of 'objects', as a whole, and the more particular concept of a 'chair'. She has developed her use of language in order to communicate, she can translate the symbols in this book, or in the picture on the wall, or in the music. These processes of perception, memory, concept formation, language and symbolization are basic cognitive processes. In addition cognitive processes underlie the ability to solve problems, to reason and to learn. To study cognition, then, is to study those structures and processes whereby human beings selectively take into their minds aspects of external events, sort out these initial impressions, either reject or store them and, finally, retrieve and use these systematically stored contents of the mind when required in order to carry out the activities of their daily lives.

To speak of 'cognitive development' can be subtly misleading in that the phrase combines both the processes and the content to which these processes are applied, suggesting that *both* develop. In fact infants and young children may well have available to them the same processes as adults; they can perceive, remember, form concepts and communicate, but the use to which they put these processes is, initially and necessarily, different from that of adults. Much of what an adult sees around him or her is familiar enough to be recognizable. While the student may not have seen that particular bird before she does recognize it as 'a bird' and may be able to categorize it more precisely as 'a seagull' or 'a starling'. The infant or young child, on the other hand, is continually being presented with totally novel stimuli. Clearly the child cannot attend to all this novel stimuli at once. The most efficient strategy would seem to be to attend to those aspects of the environment which are most salient for survival at any one time. The fact that the child's cognitive behaviour appears to be deficient when compared with that of an adult may simply reflect the fact that, in a given situation, the two are presented with differing tasks. The adult, as it were, knows her or his way around and can choose how to employ her or his cognitive powers, whereas the child has to use these powers to make sense of a largely novel environment.

However, as cognitive processes are used and as the environment becomes more comprehensible, it is possible that by the very act of trying to understand the environment the processes themselves develop. In psychology today there is considerable discussion of what develops when cognition develops. This controversy, obviously, cannot be resolved here but we should be aware that when we speak of 'cognitive development' we may be speaking of the development of the processes themselves or the development of the application of such processes to different contents, or both.

Contemporary psychology is often thought to have its roots in the 'behaviourism' of Watson (1913) and the 'neobehaviourism' of Hull (1943). This approach is characterized by limiting its enquiry to the investigation of overt behaviour; thus ruling out the study of internal processes. Any item of human behaviour, including cognition, is described as a 'response' to a 'stimulus'. The reason why a person gives a particular response to a particular stimulus was thought to be either because the two were associated in some way, that is, the response was 'conditioned', or because the appearance of this response had been rewarded previously. Experiments in discrimination learning were often used to demonstrate this. Characteristically in such experiments a rat would be presented with a choice between two stimuli, for example, a black and a white passageway. If, whenever it chose the black passageway it was rewarded, it would, ultimately, 'learn' to choose the black passageway each time. If the animal were still in the process of learning, a question of interest was whether reversing the schedules of reinforcement, so that a choice of the white passageway was rewarded, would retard the animal's learning since it had already experienced the black passageway as rewarding, or whether this reversal would make no difference as the animal had not 'learnt' to respond to black. Spence (1936), in his 'single unit' theory, argued that the process of learning was continuous, so that even if the animal were still making mistakes, reversing the schedules would retard learning as it was beginning to learn to respond to black. He predicted that an animal whose schedules had been reversed would learn to discriminate more slowly than one who had always had the same choice rewarded. Experiments at the time showed that Spence's prediction received the most support (Riley, 1968). An implication, that was not made explicit at the time, is that such incremental learning requires a 'storage'

3

system of some kind. The Kendlers (1962) then extended this work. In one of their experiments a child was presented with four cups: a large black one, a large white one, a small black one and a small white one. In the first stage of the experiment the child learnt to respond positively to one dimension, for example size, so that the large cup was positive and small one negative, but colour was ignored. In a 'reversal' shift the child had to learn, in stage 2, to respond to the same dimension but to *reverse* her or his choice so that small became positive and large negative. In a non-reversal shift in the second stage she or he changed dimension by ignoring size and concentrating on colour so that black became positive and white negative. The results showed that children below the age of six, slow-learning children and rats found non-reversal shifts easier to learn whereas older children and college students found reversal shifts easier. The Kendlers' argument was that if the older children and adults were using mediating responses such as 'size' in stage 1, all they needed to do in a reversal shift in stage 2 was to choose 'small' instead of 'large', whereas in a non-reversal shift they had to develop the new mediating response of 'colour'. On the other hand, if the young children were not using mediators but behaved as single unit theory would predict then the relative ease of the tasks should be reversed, since in the non-reversal shift all the child had to do was to associate the new stimulus 'black' with a positive response which, colour having not been involved before, was comparatively easy; whereas in a reversal shift that which had been positive had to become negative. It was this 'unlearning' which gave the younger children greatest difficulty. It therefore appeared that while non-human animals and young humans learn in a continuous, single unit fashion, older humans use an internal mediator which interposes between the stimulus and the response. The Kendlers and their associates then considered the development of mediation more closely (T.S. and H.H. Kendler and Learnard, 1962; H.H. and T.S. Kendler, 1971; T.S. Kendler and Ward, 1972). As a result of these studies they concluded (1975):

Infrahuman behaviour is consistent with the single unit continuity model . . . college students with the mediational model. The probability that a child's choice will fit one or the other depends on his age: the younger he is the more likely he is to behave according to a single unit theory, whereas the older he is

4

the more likely his performance will be consonant with the mediational model. (pp. 207–8)

In a further study of the nature of mediators (Kendler, Glasman and Ward, 1972) they compared the behaviour of three groups of pre-school children. The first group received no training, the second were trained to attend to the essential characteristics of the stimulus, for example, size or colour, and the third were trained to use the verbal label for the stimuli. After the training the second and third group were both more able to make reversal shifts in a discrimination task than were the untrained group, but the verbally trained group were the most proficient. They explained this (1975) by saying that 'the verbal label provides symbolic representation, a cognitive operator that mediates an RS. Although the perceptual differentiation may be required for this symbolic representation and may encourage its production, it does not by itself guarantee its occurrence' (p. 219). In this they drew attention to the significance of symbolization and the role of internal cognitive processes.

Over time, in psychology, interest has shifted from the study of responses to how people acquire and process 'knowledge' or 'information'. The 'information-processing' approach to cognition is, in some senses, the most intuitively obvious. The model is that of a person who perceives stimuli, stores it, retrieves it, and uses it. Thus an information-processing system (IPS) (Newell and Simon, 1972) is thought to consist of a sensory system, a response generator, a memory and a central processor. A basic assumption is that information is transformed in various ways at certain stages in its processing. The role of memory is central as is the way knowledge is represented in memory. For example, when a person remembers the concept of a 'chair' what can he or she be said to be doing? Memory can be divided into 'short-term' memory, where what has just been taken is held for a few seconds, and 'long-term' memory, the more permanent storage system. Tulving (1972) further distinguished 'episodic' from 'semantic' memory believing that these each represented a different processing system. 'Episodic' memory stores memories which can be located in time and space and refer to some particular event that happened, whereas 'semantic' memory contains generalized information about the nature of things, for example, that a chair is a type of furniture. An important question is how knowledge is represented in memory.

Here we must distinguished between the 'content' of the knowledge, for example all the features of 'a bird', and the 'code' or the *way* we express this concept, for example by the word 'bird' in English and '*oiseau*' in French; finally the 'medium' is the physical representation of a code as in written or spoken language. The information-processing approach to cognition is particularly concerned with the nature of these representations, in particular representational codes.

A person processes information from the environment by applying existing 'programs' to it in a serial, step-by-step manner and these programs are situation specific (Newell and Simon, 1972; Dawes, 1975). The information-processing approach starts from the question 'What processing routines and what kinds of internally stored information would a person need in order to generate the observed behaviour?' (Klahr, 1980, p. 128). The answer is expressed as a set of rules which could be interpreted by a computer program and therefore needs to be exact. It is thought that when environmental stimuli are processed this is done on a number of layers, each of which has a storage capacity. Initially information is received and passed to short-term memory (STM) where it will be rejected or moved to long-term memory (LTM) which

> appears to be of essentially unlimited capacity. It is organized as a network of associated concepts and propositions, and a collection of strategies and procedures. The routines of LTM control information transfer among the layers of processing, the searching of the conceptual and propositional network, and programs for the modification of LTM. (ibid., p. 129)

This approach argues that children process information in exactly the same way as adults, but that adults have better 'production systems' defined as

> a formalism for expressing how an information-processing system might respond to the momentary state of knowledge in which it finds itself. That is, how it might determine what to do next, given what it now knows. (ibid., p. 129)

On this model children both know less than adults, and are poorer at knowing what to do with what they know.

A difficulty with the information-processing model is that it can be taken to imply that 'information' and 'processing' can be independent of each other, that is that there is an objective entity called 'information'. However, it is possible that qualities in the processor may determine what, for that person, the 'information' will be. For example, expectation may distort perception in that we may see what we expect to see. Piaget developed a theory which explicitly took account of the contribution of the 'subject', that is the person who processes, and the 'object', that is the information to be processed. Piaget's view was that the child *constructs*, during the course of development, an individual understanding of the real world. Thus intelligence is interactionist in essence. What the child knows is neither determined by her or his own ideas nor wholly by the object, but rather by an interaction between the two. Piaget called this the 'invention' or 'construction' of reality, not the 'discovery' of a reality that exists 'out there' independent of the knowing subject. The child's knowledge, therefore, is neither based wholly on experience (empiricism), nor on pre-existing mental structures (rationalism). For example, the child could not have *learnt* the principle of conservation empirically (see p. 83). It is a concept that is seldom directly taught or even mentioned. Nor was such a concept necessary for the child to experience the world at all and, indeed, the child's early exchanges with the world do not make use of such a concept. Similarly if A is bigger than B and B than C then the fact that A is bigger than C is true by definition and needs no empirical verification, but the child was found, by Piaget, not to use such transitive inferences initially. Nevertheless, over time, the child moves from a prelogical state to a logical one through, according to Piaget, the constructive processes of cognitive growth.

For Piaget, knowledge was inextricably linked with development. The source of development was integral to the nature of knowledge itself, since for Piaget 'to know' meant that the person had constructed a cognitive structure. In so far as an existing structure proves inadequate in the subject's dialogue with the object, so it would need to be transformed into a new structure. Thus cognitive development was conceived of as the construction by the child of those logical structures by means of which reality is comprehended. It was not thought to be the development of the means by which the person is able to produce ever closer copies of, or approximations to, reality.

Since, for Piaget, the epistemological question, 'What is

7

knowledge?' and the psychological question, 'How do we come to know?' were closely related, he developed a general theory of cognitive development on the basis of his epistemology. He argued that all human cognition is rooted in biology and that human knowledge is the result of an evolutionary process.

He maintained, first, that man, like all other biological phenomena, has a characteristic internal organization which determines how people respond to external stimuli; secondly, that this determines man's unique 'mode of functioning' which is invariant or unchangeable. A person when faced with environmental stimuli will attempt to make sense of it by using her or his existing structures, that is, to 'assimilate' it. If the existing structures are inadequate for the task they will have to change or 'accommodate' themselves to take account of the new information. The result of using the invariant functions of assimilation and accommodation is that the person's structures are changed or 'adapted'. Thus, Piaget's third point was that the invariant functions gave rise to the 'variant', or changeable, 'structures', that is, the person's cognitive abilities at any one time, through organism/environment interaction. This development was thought to start with action since, for Piaget, the source of knowledge was action. He argued that at first the infant merely acts when she or he comes into contact with reality; soon, the initial reflex or random actions are co-ordinated into sets, such as the set of actions related to sucking. These sets of co-ordinated actions form 'schemes'. The various schemes which a person has developed at any one time in turn form a 'structure'. There is therefore, according to Piaget, a developmental sequence from reflex scheme, to sensori-motor (or action) scheme, to structure.

The structures and their component schemes were said to change over time through the process of 'equilibration'. Briefly, this means that if a subject finds that her (or his) present schemes are inadequate to cope with a new situation which has arisen in the environment so that she cannot 'assimilate' the new information, she will be thrown, cognitively, into disequilibrium. She will then 'accommodate' her schemes so that she can take in the information and thus adapt, or reconstruct, her structures. Here Piaget's belief in the interpenetration of organism and environment can be seen. The subject is not dominated by the object, or vice versa, but rather the subject's internal organization enables her to comprehend objects, and the properties of the objects cause the subject to reorganize her internal organization. Once the structure is reorganized equilibrium is restored. Equilibrium, however, is not static; it represents 'an active system of compensation' (Inhelder, 1962, p. 28), and is indicative of the self-regulating aspects of the organism as well as its activity. There is no final point of equilibrium. Throughout life the transformation of structures will continue. The above five postulates: internal organization, invariant functions, variant structures, equilibration and organism/environment interaction were fundamental to Piaget's theory.

The process of equilibration gives rise to the 'stages' of cognitive development which represent different forms of action by the subject towards the objects in the environment. These have been given excessive weight by popularizers of Piaget's theories. In one of his earliest works Piaget introduced these stages thus:

> The question of reasoning and particularly of contradiction in the child is closely bound up with the problem of modality or of the different planes of reality on which the child uses his thought . . . there may be several realities for the child and these realities may be equally real in turn instead of being arranged in a hierarchy as with us. . . . Four stages can be picked out in the evolution of modality. The first lasts till the age of 2–3, the second extends from 2–3 to 7–8, the third from 7–8 to 11–12 and fourth begins at this age. During the first stage reality may be said to be simply and solely what is desired. Freud's 'pleasure principle' deforms and refashions the world to its liking. The second stage marks the appearance of two heterogeneous but equal realities – the world of play and the world of observation. The third marks the beginning of hierarchical arrangements, and the fourth marks the completion of this hierarchy, thanks to the introduction of a new plane – that of formal thought and logical assumptions. (Piaget, 1924/1926, pp. 244–6)

By this Piaget meant that the prelogical, magical, world of the child develops, in the third stage, into a form of 'concrete' logic by means of which the child can order events in various ways provided they are practically present for the child (see p. 106). In the fourth stage the child can use abstract thought enabling her or him to transcend the here and now and consider possibilities as well as actualities (see p. 109).

9

Several factors were thought to affect development from stage to stage (Piaget, 1972c/1974). Firstly, biological factors; secondly, equilibration factors by which Piaget meant self-regulatory factors which he said 'will depend on circumstances as much as epigenetic potentialities' and hence give rise to individual differences within groups; thirdly, social factors. Here he distinguished between the universals of social behaviour and particular forms which are limited to certain societies, and opposed universal social factors to individual regulatory factors. Finally, he saw factors of education and cultural transmission as being responsible for differences between social groups.

Although Piaget does discuss cognitive development in terms of the qualitative differences between the thinking characteristic of one stage and that of another, to see his theory as, fundamentally, a stage theory would be a mistake. A child may well operate at one stage for one form of understanding and at another for another. While an individual child's thinking may be broadly characterized by a stage description Piaget, in his later works, preferred to model cognitive development by a spiral, thus emphasizing that the child's progression is continuous rather than stepwise, as stage theory implies.

Pascual-Leone (1980) argued that Piagetian and information-processing approaches complement each other but that both fail to give sufficient consideration to individual differences. He therefore maintained that if there were internal structures independent of, and prior to, the utilization of strategies required for the solution of particular tasks then a study of these internal structures would require (1) Piagetian experimental designs; (2) the experimental manipulation of types of tasks; (3) the experimental manipulation of types of subjects; and (4) a method of analysis which would enable the researcher to specify exactly what strategies certain types of subject would use on certain types of task. The study of cognitive development may follow this scheme in the future.

Piagetian theory has led to a great deal of subsequent research and educators have hoped to apply it to classroom practice. It is, obviously, not the only approach to cognitive development, although it is probably the most inclusive to date. As Beilin (1980) commented, 'If one considers within developmental psychology the contemporary alternatives to Piaget's theory one finds relatively few major adversaries although there are a number of minor ones' (p. 245). One such alternative is skill theory which defines cognitive development as 'the construction of hierarchically ordered collections of specific skills' (Fischer, 1980, p. 477). This approach argues that as the person will be called upon to use different skills for different tasks in different environmental contexts one must expect unequal development, not regular structural changes. Cognition is seen as the processes which enable the person to control variation in what she or he does and thinks. So,

> as cognitive development progresses infants first control varia-
> tions in their sensori-motor actions, then children control
> variations in their own representations, and finally adolescents
> or adults control variations in their own abstractions. (p. 481)

In doing this the person develops 'sets'. An infant shaking a rattle has an appropriate set of behaviours for this task and a skill is defined as 'a unit of behaviour composed of one or more sets' (p. 482). These skills are said to differ from the Piagetian schemes in that the environment is an intrinsic part of a skill – i.e. the skill will refer to shaking a *rattle* – whereas the schemes are more general in application. This, Fischer believes, accounts for the unevenness of development in that if skills are specific to environments or objects then discontinuity in development would be what would be expected. Conservation of weight would occur after conservation of substance because if the contribution of the concepts of *weight* and *substance* determined the sequence, not the general scheme of *conservation*, then uneven development would be expected, not the even development predicted by a structural analysis.

The child's skills, but not the child in general, are thought to develop through seven levels and the child may operate at different levels for different skills. Thus the child's performance can be described in a profile of skill attainment but not in a stage description as 'pre-operational' or 'operational'. The levels are divided into cycles of four levels, called tiers, of which the first, representing levels 1–4, is the sensori-motor; levels 4–7 are characterized by representational sets; and levels 7–10 by abstract sets. Each level is thought to subsume the sets from earlier tiers. Skills are transformed to more advanced skills by five 'transformation rules'. The first two, 'interco-ordination' and 'compounding', result in the development of new skills by the combination of current ones, with the former relating to change between levels and the latter within a level. 'Focusing' models slight shifts between skills, and 'substitution' certain cases of generalization. The final rule of 'differentiation' shows the existing sets breaking up into new subsets. These transformations take place when required by *both* the organism and the environment, so that the new skill must be appropriate for a given environment and environmental properties may cause a person to juxtapose the use of two skills and hence explore the relationship between them.

This view of development implies that development will be uneven across task areas since 'The level, or step within a level, that an individual attains on a task is affected by so many environmental factors that he or she could not possibly perform at the same level or step on all tasks' (p. 513). In addition individuals will both develop expertise in different areas of skill and will follow different paths in attaining the same skill. Fischer points out two current limitations of skill theory. First, the difficulty of defining areas of skill or 'skill domain' and, second, the process by which skills are accessed, i.e. it is difficult to explain why a person uses, or fails to use, a skill which they have in their repertoire.

This approach stresses the contribution of the environment and underlines the fact that a person may have attained one level in one skill domain and another in another. It differs from Piaget in that, in skill theory, the skills of one level are subsumed into the next whereas in Piagetian theory the cognitive structures are themselves reconstructed as the result of the equilibratory process. In addition one can distinguish between the knowledge that a person has acquired and the way the person uses that knowledge when problem solving. This latter form of knowledge requires the development of 'procedural' skills which may have to be learned separately from other forms of knowledge gathering.

The final approach to cognitive development and that which is, currently, the most popular, stresses the importance of the person being able to 'think about thinking' or 'metacognition'. Flavell (1976, 1978; Flavell and Wellman, 1977) argued that for this to be possible people must first know the kinds of situation in which intentional cognition is possible; secondly understand what they can do, themselves, to influence their learning and memory; thirdly to be able to analyse the relevant characteristics of the task so as to know how easy or difficult it is; and finally to be able to find the appropriate strategies to use when faced with a particular type of task. Learning could be greatly enhanced if the learner could be made aware of these aspects of metacognition. There have been some attempts to train people to use metacognition and the results are encouraging. Butterfield, Wambold and Belmont (1973) trained retarded adolescents to use a strategy to aid memory retrieval and found that, after training, their performance was better than non-retarded adolescents who had no training. In some way this approach is similar to the old notion that children needed to learn how to learn as Norman, Gentner and Stevens (1976) ask,

> Why do we not attempt to teach some basic cognitive skills such as how to organize one's knowledge, how to learn, how to solve problems, how to correct errors in understanding. These strike us as basic components which ought to be taught along with the content matter. (p. 194)

Therefore, at present, we have a number of approaches to cognitive development all of which accept that there are differences in the cognitive processing of children and adults but do not agree how these differences should best be characterized. In this book, while various approaches will be referred to, the Piagetian model will be most in evidence, but it should be remembered that it is only one of several ways of describing and attempting to explain cognitive development.

Applying theory to practice

If education is seen as being, at least in part, the intentional transmission of knowledge and understanding in order to develop the powers of thought of the recipient, then an understanding of the process of cognitive development would seem to be an essential prerequisite for such an enterprise. However, although there are some educational implications following from our understanding of the characteristic modes of thought of individuals of various ages, the connection between theory and practice is neither conceptually nor operationally clear.

While the experimental study of children may show that when carrying out type X tasks successfully, they use type Y strategies, which presuppose the existence of type Z structures, what the educator is expected to do with such a piece of information is not implicit in the description of the children's behaviour. Many possibilities exist. It may, or may not, be true that success in certain tasks will follow on the development of the necessary strategies. However, how is this development best fostered? It may well follow that in the absence of certain structures children will not be able to tackle certain tasks and this has implications for the selection of curriculum content, but such decisions are static in that they enable the educator to make day-to-day decisions but give little information on how to aid development itself. If isolated aspects of a theory are selected and applied to classroom practice then it is unlikely that they will have much influence, simply because they are part of a wider theory and only have meaning in such a context. There is therefore no necessary connection between theories of cognitive development and educational practice. Links may be hypothesized, but then such hypotheses need to be empirically tested and, if found to be valid, educational practice modified.

A major difficulty in applying psychologists' understanding of cognitive development directly to education is that the former are concerned with the *processes* whereby we come to know, whereas curriculum-designers often start from the *outcomes* of such processes, as in seeking to develop literacy or numeracy. At times there is an implicit assumption that practising the skills which define the outcome of the learning process – for example carrying out arithmetical procedures or deciphering the printed word – will facilitate the process itself. Such an implication may be unwarranted. It is possible that an understanding of cognition and its development will aid the educator both to devise curricula whose contents are more appropriate for individuals at certain developmental stages. It may also enable her to arrange for pupils to have the experiences and practise the skills which are thought to be a precondition for developing certain forms of human understanding. The outcomes of these forms of understanding have traditionally formed the basis for educational instruction. However, such decisions are educational, not psychological, decisions. The psychologists, who study the development of cognition, can only report what they find. The use to which such findings are put are the responsibility of those with different areas of expertise. In other words, one cannot move from an 'is' to an 'ought'. Thus whenever educational implications are discussed in this book such a discussion should be read as exploratory and, essentially, tentative.

2

Infancy (0–2 years)

At any one time the human adult's knowledge of the world is the result of both external stimuli, potentially detectable by the senses, and an internal reception, recognition and appraisal of such stimuli. Cognitive development is the development of the processes by means of which the sensations received by the senses are categorized and responded to. Such processes result in individual constructions of reality within a context of shared cultural and social meanings. By the time maturity is reached the adult has developed categories of understanding, or ways of interrogating reality, some of which are held in common with all other humans, some with a few others and some, possibly, with no others. One person's world will be similar to another's to the extent that both detect and process external stimuli similarly. Maturity marks the culmination of such development, birth its inception. The human infant, as a product of evolutionary adaptation, begins by responding to the perceived environment using pre-existing patterns of response which will both effect subsequent development and themselves be modified by it.

The capacities of the newborn infant

At birth human infants are ready to start this process of cognitive growth. Their senses are not only able to receive external stimuli, in that they can see, hear, taste, smell and feel, but also they can pay selective attention to just these aspects of events which are of relevance for newborn humans. Recently, it has been suggested (Trevarthen, 1979b) that infants also possess a rudimentary sense of intentionality and interpersonal sharing. If human infants were not able to pay selective attention to stimuli they would be overwhelmed by a barrage of sensations, and indeed this was once believed to be the case (James, 1890). Such a view derived from the empiricist notion that at birth the mind was like a blank slate and would be formed by experience. This image implied a decorticated baby capable only of reflex responses and ignored the influence of evolutionary adaptation on the organization of the human brain. However, it now seems obvious that the means by which external stimuli are received, and hence experienced, will influence the nature of such experience. For humans the means of receiving stimuli are their sense receptors and brains, which in accordance with their own organization make sense of such sensations. Therefore the brains of human infants will intervene between all the possible sensations to be processed and the actual sensations which are attended to. This does not imply that at birth this organization is fixed and immutable, leaving experience with no role to play. It appears that certain aspects of this organization are indeed present at birth as the legacy of evolution, and are thus a precondition for having experience at all, but other aspects of the brain's organization are derived from such experience. Just as the digestive system is capable of digesting some substances and not others, so the infant brain will filter stimuli. To further the analogy, infants will develop well physically if they are adequately nourished, less well if under-fed and will die if poisoned. None of these outcomes relate directly to the mode of functioning of the digestive system which can only digest or refuse to digest. Infants' cognitive development too will be influenced by the nature of the experiences available for their brains to work on. What is considerably less clear is the extent to which experience and organization respectively are influential for any one individual; in other words what their relative weighting is for the cognitive growth of the person. This is a problem to which we will return.

It was Wolff's pioneering paper (1959), based on his own observations, that drew the attention of psychologists to the fact that a newborn infant's behaviour was organized and exhibited stable patterns. In particular he drew attention to the existence of different states of arousal, pointing out that the infant can be deeply asleep with only slight movement, half asleep with some movement, awake and alert with eyes open, and awake and crying. It is in the awake-and-alert state, when need and satiety are balanced, that the infant is capable of engaging in the precursors of cognitive activity such as attending to specific stimuli or tracking an object. Infants have been found to vary in the amount of time they spend in this state. If they are ignored at such times, or stimulated when they are sleepy or distressed, interpersonal stimulation will either be lacking or be a frustrating impingement. Thus the only experiences available, when infants are most receptive, will be those which arise from the inanimate environment, and the resulting cognitive organization will arguably be different from one which results from interpersonal interaction.

Visually, infants are remarkably sensitive, being able to discriminate between patterned and plain figures, circularity and linearity, and the wavelengths that correspond to blue, green, yellow and red (Kagan, 1979). Since they cannot speak, finding out that they have these visual capacities involves using indices of discrimination, as in the work of Fantz or the ingenious experimental techniques of Bower and his colleagues. Fantz's earliest experiment with humans was reported (1958) shortly after Wolff's paper. In it he used the paired-comparison technique in which the infant was shown a pair of stimuli selected from a range consisting of different shapes, colours and patterns. The amount of time an infant spent looking at a particular member of each pair was called a 'preference'. Infants under 2 months were found to prefer a striped pattern, with this being replaced by a bull's-eye after 2 months. Strictly speaking what Fantz demonstrated was not visual preference but the ability to discriminate between the stimuli, since if the infant could not discriminate between the two consistently lengthened regard for one would not occur. Later studies of visual acuity (Fantz, 1966; Fantz et al., 1962) showed that pattern recognition was extremely competent throughout the first six months and that, not surprisingly, stimulus conditions such as illumination affected acuity. Adults often show infants a toy held at a point beyond their range of vision, i.e. approximately 8 inches at birth, and then conclude that the infant cannot focus when it is the adult who is failing to anticipate the infant's visual requirements. Infants were also found to pay selectively greater attention to patterns which were face-like. Fantz interpreted this as evidence for their greater interest in complexity, so that they are interested in faces mainly because they are complex, but as a consequence their attention is drawn to objects of importance to them. Fantz's conclusion, after many years of studying infant visual activity, was that they could both see and discriminate patterns at birth and that their attention to such patterns was selective.

Fantz's work stimulated a considerable amount of subsequent research into infant visual perception. Carpenter (1975) studied infants aged 1 to 8 weeks. In one experiment she showed each infant an abstract facial form, a shop-model's face and the mother's face. None of the faces moved. The infants looked longer at the first two than at the mother's from which they appeared to withdraw. An unmoving maternal face may have been perceived as incongruous and hence the infants looked away. In another experiment the infants were found to look longer at the mother's face than they did at a stranger's but showed distress when the mother's face was paired with the stranger's voice. These findings suggest that infants are able to discriminate between familiar and unfamiliar faces and voices, and anticipate maternal activity at a very young age.

Bower *et al.* (1970a) showed that infants a few days old will attempt to defend themselves against an object which appears to be going to hit them. Ball and Tronick (1971), following Bower *et al.*, demonstrated that infants would not show concern when the object's trajectory indicated that it would miss them, which implies some very early understanding of the radial direction of moving objects. The infants were also found to be genuinely able to see that the objects were coming closer and not merely to be reacting to the retinal expansion of the object. To test this the infants were shown a small object approaching close to them and a large object which stopped further away, with the result that the retinal image of the two objects was identical. The infants were found to respond defensively to the small object which came close and could have hit them but ignored the larger object which stopped, safely, further away. Both objects would, at that moment, have appeared to be the same size had the infants not been able to take distance into account.

Salapatek (1975), in a full review of infant pattern perception, sounds a note of caution by suggesting that humans and other species have cortical units which are highly sensitive to certain features of objects' contours and therefore human infants would be expected to show such sensitivity. However, the cortex develops significantly after birth and the development of visual perception may be very dependent on the infant being exposed to visual stimuli at this period of development. He does not believe that the initial sensitivity of the infant implies that a 'mind' is at work, in that the discrimination the infants show may be the result of connections between cortical units and reflex responses. Rather he suggests that 'a defensive response to a geometrically expanding object, or to depth at an edge, or visual orientation toward a face ... could be innate, reflexive and never require encoding' (pp. 172–3).

Infants' auditory perception seems to be equally acute and selective. Newborns have been found to look towards a sound (Wertheimer, 1961); their heart rate responds to changes in sound intensity (Steinschneider *et al.*, 1966), and by the age of 3 weeks they show distress if their mother's voice does not seem to issue from her mouth (Aronson and Rosenbloom, 1971); they expect by then to hear their mother's voice coming from a specific place. They have also been found to show differential responses to sounds of different frequencies. Lower frequencies are more likely to be responded to and have been found to inhibit distress (Birns, 1965) while higher frequencies may cause the infant to 'freeze'. Of particular interest are suggestions that infants are able to pay particular attention to linguistic data as if they are sensitized to this from amongst the mass of sounds that assail them. Condon and Sander (1974) tested infants of 12 hours old, all born in the United States, by playing them tapes of spoken English and Chinese, making tapping noises and saying single vowel sounds. An adult also spoke to them. The infants responded by movement to all the forms of continuous speech but ignored the taps and the single vowels. Eimas *et al.* (1971) tested slightly older infants of 1 month and 4 months and found that they could discriminate between the consonants /b/ and /p/. They concluded:

The results strongly indicate that infants as young as one month of age are not only responsive to speech sounds and able to make fine discriminations but are ... able to sort acoustic variations of adult phonemes into categories with relatively limited exposure to speech. (p. 306)

In addition infants appear to respond to speech sounds which are not those of their native language (Eimas, 1975; Streeter, 1976), suggesting that such selective attention was acquired during the evolution of the species enabling the infant to respond to *any* natural language and, possibly, appearing simultaneously with the appearance of language itself. Researchers who have studied the ability of rhesus monkeys to discriminate consonants (Morse and Snowdon, 1975; Waters and Wilson, 1976) have found that they too seem able to make such discriminations and therefore this ability may be one which the human infant shares with other primates and which would, therefore, have had to develop before the differentiation of the human species from the non-human primates.

Human language also requires the listener to realize that although words and strings of words consist of discrete sounds they can be grouped, and it is these groups that carry meaning. Demany *et al.* (1977) showed that infants were able to perceive rhythm in that, like adults, when exposed to a series of identical tone bursts, they did not code them as a single sound repeated several times but chunked them into subjectively ordered segments based on the intervals between the bursts. Thus they could discriminate between bursts having the form /. ../ and the form /.. ./.

The other sensory modalities have been less well researched but infants have been shown to be able to turn away from odours that adults rank as unpleasant (Bower, 1982), which means that they can locate the position of the odour, presumably on the basis of the fact that it reaches each nostril at a slightly different time. Bower concludes from this that, 'the capacity to locate position on the basis of olfactory time differences is probably built into the structure of the organism' (p. 19). MacFarlane (1975) demonstrated that by 8 to 10 days an infant could distinguish between a breast pad worn by his or her mother and one which was either unused or had been worn by a stranger. In his experiment the mother's pad was lowered over one side of the infant's head and either the stranger's or a clean one over the other side. The infant's ability to discriminate a familiar from an unfamiliar odour was judged by whether they turned their heads more towards the mother's pad or towards the other pads or distributed their head turns equally. Seventeen out of twenty infants were found to turn more towards the mother's pad than a clean one and twenty-five out of thirty-two to turn more towards the mother's than a stranger's. The results were taken to indicate that they could distinguish between odours and 'preferred' the mother's pad.

With respect to touch, infants appear to 'expect' objects to be tangible. Bower *et al.* (1970b) performed a series of experiments which demonstrated this. A visual illusion was used to trick infants into believing that they could see a real object but when they tried to touch it there was in fact no object present. Bower (1982) described the infants' behaviour thus:

> It was found that all newborn infants touched and grasped real objects without any sign of being disturbed. They also grasped at empty air when no visible object was present. The virtual object, however, produced a howl as soon as the infants' hands went to the location of the intangible object. (p. 123)

Given that newborns have the above capacities a question of some interest is the extent to which they are able to co-ordinate them. They can look towards a sound, an odour source and a part of their bodies which has been touched. They also expect objects which look real to be tangible and will protect themselves from objects which appear to be about to hit them. These co-ordinations do not seem to be the result of learning but rather to be present at birth as a result of evolutionary adaptation. In addition the fact that infants are able to distinguish between familiar stimuli indicates that they have a basic capacity to remember, even if it is no more than 'recognition' memory (i.e. the ability to recognize an object as familiar when they see it but not be able to recall it in its absence). The ability to 'recall' requires the infant to have some capacity to represent the absent object or event internally and hence would not develop until the end of this period, with the development of the ability to create internal representations. However, by about the age of 2 the two basic processes of recognition and recall have been found to have developed (Goldberg *et al.*, 1974).

In the early weeks of life it looks as if anything is possible, cognitively, for the normal healthy infant has considerable cognitive potential. Infants have available both the sensory equipment and the cognitive organization to attend to all those aspects of the human environment of relevance for their existence. As the months pass, selective exposure to certain experiences will mean that all the possibilities will not be actualized. Development is thus both loss and gain. An adult's construction of reality is the actualization of one spectrum of possibilities and, by its existence, renders impossible the emergence of others.

Cognitive development during the first two years

Newborn infants filter the stimuli they are exposed to. This is a necessary precondition for cognition. However, cognition can only be said to begin once the infant is able, even in a rudimentary way, to compare the incoming stimuli with stored information, or schemes, built up from previous exposures to stimuli. By means of such comparisons infants are able to recognize the new input as familiar, novel or discrepant and in the light of this appraisal behave towards it in a regular or rule-governed way. It was Piaget (1936a/1952, 1936b/1954) who first both described and developed a theory of the course and nature of infant cognition based on observations of his three children. Piaget was a 'constructivist' who believed that in development each new level is always a *reorganization* of the previous one; it is not merely the result of adding new knowledge, or facts, to the previous level or levels. Development comes about when a stable set of structures or organizational forms of mental activity are challenged by either an external or internal event or change which they cannot cope with. This sets up 'disequilibrium'. New structures are constructed which are able to cope. Equilibrium is restored and a new developmental level is reached.

Piaget thought there were three stages, or periods, of development apparent in the first two years and that these were subdivided into six sub-stages. During this period infants were thought to construct their cognitive sub-structures which would serve as a point of departure for later development. Infants were thought by him to move from a stage of *reflexes* and spontaneous movements through *habits* to *sensori-motor* or practical intelligence as such.

0–6 weeks

At this age infants are characterized by acting first and thinking afterwards. For example an initially random action leads infants to bring their hands to their mouths, thus eliciting the reflex action of sucking. They will then seek to repeat this originally unintentional action of thumb-sucking because it has been found to be 'profitable', in Piaget's terminology, or 'pleasurable', in Freud's. For Piaget the origins of intelligence were to be found in *action*, which has obvious implications for infants whose actions are limited through handicaps of one kind or another.

6 weeks to 4 or 5 months

Now the original reflex actions are co-ordinated into 'primary circular reactions', habits or routines. Piaget did not believe that infants at this stage were capable of 'intention'; that is they could not think what they would do and then do it. Thus he did not feel that their behaviour was 'intelligent'.

> Habit is still not the same as intelligence. An elementary 'habit' is based on a general sensori-motor scheme within which there is not yet, from the subject's point of view, any differentiation between means and ends. The end in question is attained only by a necessary succession of movements which lead to it, without being able to distinguish either an end pursued from the start or means chosen from among various possible schemes. In an act of intelligence, on the other hand, the end is established from the outset and pursued after a search for the appropriate means. (Piaget and Inhelder, 1966b/1969, p. 9)

4 to 8 or 9 months

Intentionality now appears as the infant seeks 'to make interesting sights last' (Piaget, 1936a/1952). Thus, if infants notice that kicking the side of the cot will make a dangling toy move, they will continue kicking. These intentional actions are called by Piaget 'secondary circular reactions'. However, the infants are not yet able to distinguish between the means and the end and therefore overgeneralize the effects of a single action, believing, for example, that kicking the side of the cot will bring about a repetition of all the interesting sights and sounds that they wish to experience again.

9–12 months

During this period infants begin to take more account of the connection between a specific action and a specific effect. They become able to keep an end in mind, such as finding a toy, while they are seeking for it and are not distracted by the intervening actions of looking under a table or behind a chair. This means that infants are now able to keep a representation of a desired end in their minds while carrying out the entirely different actions which constitute the means of attaining that end. Furthermore practical intelligence has developed in so far as infants can invent new ways of achieving their aims, since seeking a toy is unlikely to require exactly the same means on any two occasions. This ability to make intentional, novel yet appropriate responses indicates the presence of intelligence.

12–18 months

The competent newborn has now become the curious and exploring toddler. When infants themselves become the active investigators of interesting sights and happenings within their own environment, 'tertiary circular reactions' appear which act directly upon objects. Novelty is sought for its own sake and infants' greatest reward is for their actions to have had an effect on the animate and inanimate objects which constitute their world.

18–24 months

Now direct, novelty-seeking experiments are more likely to be replaced by hypothesized actions. Infants think before they act and become able to consider an action sequence in their minds without necessarily carrying it out in the real world. For this to be possible the infant must be able to create mental representations with, at least, a minimum of mental imagery. Therefore the stage of perceptually dominated sensori-motor intelligence, based on action, gives way to the conceptual world of the pre-operational child.

In addition to describing the infants' capacity for intelligent action, Piaget considered their actual knowledge of the world in one of his earliest books, *The Construction of Reality in the Child* (1936b/1954). In this he discussed infants' practical understanding of the properties of objects and of space, time and causality. His interest was in infants' actions and practical intelligence, not in their thoughts or ideas. The argument was that the construction of categories, or ways of interrogating reality, enabled the sensori-motor infants to organize reality in a particular way.

During the first two years infants move from seeing themselves as the centre of reality, simply because they do not differentiate the self from the non-self, to realizing that they are objects within a world of objects which have certain properties and which are regulated by certain causal laws. One of the earliest distinctions infants must make is the distinction between 'me' and 'not me'. Then they have to discover various aspects of the 'not me', one of which is the independent existence of inanimate objects. Piaget believed that, at first, the object is not distinguished from the act of looking, so that if the object disappears the infant continues to look in the place where it disappeared but would not institute a search. At the next developmental stage there would be some attempt to search, but if a cloth, in full view of the infant, were to be placed over the object the infant would immediately abandon the search. Following this it became possible to search for an object which had been hidden behind a screen. However, if the object was not found behind screen A the infants would continue to seek it there even if subsequently they watched the experimenter hide it behind screen B. By their second year they would search for an object in a particular place if it had been put there when they could see exactly what was happening, but if the experimenter closed a hand over the object before putting it in its hiding place the infants would look for it in the experimenter's hand. Finally, at about 18 months, they would search for the object in all possible hiding places, showing that they could now conceptualize it as separate from themselves and as having properties of its own.

In order to develop an understanding of the properties of objects infants need to have some conception of space, time and causality. Piaget argued that, initially, their notion of *space* is fragmentary, with objects seeming to come and go at will. Later they realize that their own bodies are the centre of what they see or feel but not that moving objects have trajectories which are independent of their action upon them. Once infants begin to look behind or under objects for a toy which has been hidden it is clear that they are beginning to realize that space is, in a sense, a container within which things can continue to be. This insight is shortly followed by the realization that space is separate from the action of the self and objects begin to be considered as independent entities. Finally the infants are able to structure space and therefore become able to return to a departure point or make detours.

During the first two years the infants have very little notion of *time* beyond a vestigial understanding based on an appreciation of a period 'before' and 'after' daily activities such as feeding, bathing or sleeping. However, their understanding of *causality* does show development from the earliest stage, when they appear to believe that their movements are responsible for everything that happens around them. Piaget called this stage 'magical phenomenist causality', by which he meant that the infant believes that anything can happen and any events which occur in sequence are seen to be causally linked. Later they move to the more mature realization that their own movements have certain effects but that not all that happens is caused by them.

Thus Piaget's view is that mankind's fundamental categories of understanding, by which we order the sensations bombarding us, are neither innate nor solely the result of experience. Rather they are constructed in the course of coming to terms with the particular environmental events to which infants are exposed. During this early period, in the short space of two years, Piaget saw the child as moving from reflexes to insight. This stage ends with the development of language and the ability to use symbols.

Since Piaget's pioneering work other psychologists have added to and modified his theories. Bower (1979, 1982) suggested that infants before 5 months of age are considerably more competent than Piaget believed. He argued that it is important to distinguish between changes due to learning and changes due to development. Development was seen as the result of interaction between the genes and the environment (by which he means the 'psychological' environment composed of both objective external reality and the individual's subjective interpretation of this). Infants' genes do not, necessarily, determine development; rather their particular expression will depend on the environment so that there will be different routes to development. Bower's argument is thus a version of the one that heredity predisposes and the environment precipitates; that is, culture maximizes, or minimizes, the biologically given. He believes that the infant starts from in-built abstract rules such as 'The world is orderly' or 'The world is ordered in three dimensions' and that these are then differentiated by the infant to solve the special problems encountered in a particular environment. Thus he suggests that cognitive development is 'a process by which the general becomes specific, in which the abstract is differentiated' (Bower, 1982, p. 253). This is the reverse of Piaget's view of development as that which moves from the concrete action to the abstract rule.

Throughout his works the picture Piaget gives of the human infant is essentially one of a solitary individual constructing the categories of human knowledge by acting upon inanimate objects. Truly such an infant would believe, with Descartes, that awareness of thought is proof of existence. Human beings, however, are members of a social species and while it may be true that the infant moves from the self to the social, it is equally possible that the movement is in the opposite direction, i.e. that the infant discovers the self from the experience of being in relationship with another and that proof of existence, rather than being internally validated, develops out of an initial awareness of being the recipient of the attention of others. Thus the human infant would be social from birth and pre-adapted to develop within a context of shared understanding. If this were the case, then cognitive development could be expected to be influenced by the infant's social interactions as well as by the types of experience described by Piaget.

Trevarthen (1979a) has argued that human infants are social beings at birth, ready to interact with others of their own kind. Having observed, and filmed, the interactive behaviour of mothers and infants, he maintained: 'The patterns of intersubjective exchange between two month old babies and their mothers show that conscious sharing and a representation of processes in an I–you relationship are innate in the human brain' (p. 210). Trevarthen points out that as infants grow older, they do not just learn the properties of objects but also seek to share their experiences with other people. This too indicates that 'fundamental structures for co-operative understanding of the world, unlike anything in any other species, are innate. . . '. He concludes that 'research with infants strongly supports the idea of a natural evolutionary origin for human consciousness, interpersonal mental life and the co-operative intentions that make cultural development possible' (pp. 210–12). Trevarthen, in a decade of research into infant behaviour, has showed (1979b) that they react differently to physical objects and people, seeking to grasp, chew, kick or use the former whereas

27

they attempt to communicate with people by 'expressive movements' (p. 323). He has studied in detail the synchrony exhibited by both mothers and infants when they interact, stressing the motivation of the infant to engage in such exchanges and that often they both lead and conclude them. For him one of the prime motivations of infant behaviour is co-operation with as well as mastery of objects in the environment and it is the motive for co-operation which regulates mental development (Trevarthen, 1982). Therefore cognitive development can only be understood as 'a fluctuation of innate motives for affectionate and co-operative action with others and a progressive building of intentions that give expression to these motives' (p. 102).

Trevarthen's view would suggest that the categories of human knowledge are not just constructed by the infant but are constructed within the context of human intersubjectivity, a position supported by the Newsons (1976). They agree with Piaget that knowledge arises from interactions between the subject, i.e. the infant, and objects but add that 'the object with which the human infant interacts most often, and most effectively, particularly in the earliest stages of development, is almost invariably another human being' (J. and E. Newson, 1976, p. 85). Therefore they see cognitive development as being, essentially, the result of the interactions between the innately social human infant and other humans who have already developed the relevant forms of understanding. Infants seem to seek to share their 'knowledge' with their care-givers and in these initial exchanges, in which the care-givers treat the infants as if they do indeed comprehend more than they do, cognitive development takes root.

For example Décarie (1978) demonstrated that through realizing the individuality and permanence of the mother the infant begins to appreciate the permanence of inanimate objects, a finding supported by Bell (1970) who found that person-permanence usually preceded an understanding of object-permanence. Paraskevopoulos and Hunt's study (1971) showed that infants in an orphanage with a high infant/care-giver ratio achieved object-permanence earlier than did those in a less-well-staffed municipal orphanage. It is probable that the increased social interaction in the former was responsible for this if only because, with more adults to care for them, the infants would have a more stimulating environment in general.

Beilin (1971) argued that Piaget did not distinguish between genetically transmitted general structures, which have evolved as the species has evolved, and which would, for example, determine that more abstract formulations would follow upon practical experiences, and 'specific' structures of thought, such as the ability to conserve or use transitive inferences, which might or might not occur depending on the environment since they could be constructed from the elements available in a particular culture. Thus for Beilin general and specific structures have different origins and should not both be seen as universal. Only the species-specific general structures were thought to have that characteristic. Scarr-Salapatek (1976) maintained that infant intelligence is different in kind from later intelligence. She saw sensori-motor skills as similar to those of the great apes and the Old World monkeys and argued that this form of intelligence developed early in our primate past, i.e. before human beings separated from the hypothesized ancestor we share with non-human primates. Sensori-motor intelligence therefore has been subjected to longer and stronger natural selection than the later forms of intelligence, which may be peculiar to *Homo sapiens*, and shows less individual variation, i.e. infants are, in terms of intelligence, more like each other than are adults. It follows that human infants are born with a 'preadaptive responsiveness to certain learning opportunities' (Scarr-Salapatek, 1976, p. 194), as exemplified by, for example, hand–eye co-ordination, whose emergence is thought to be controlled by the genes since even blind infants will start to 'look at' their hands at the same age as sighted infants (Freedman, 1974).

The origins of language in infancy

Although language development begins at about the age of 2 and its inception marks the end of infancy, it would be a mistake to conclude that infancy has no significance for the development of the capacity to transmit meaning verbally. On the contrary, the process which culminates in the production and comprehension of verbal signs is rooted in infant behaviour and experience. From the moment of birth mothers speak to their infants and the infants appear to go through several distinct stages before being able to speak back. Dore (1974) listed four such stages. In the first, called *prelinguistic communication*, the infant merely communicates hunger, pain, tiredness, etc., by striking 'orectic attitudes'. Here one may question whether this is indeed 'communication', which implies intention, or whether it is more a matter of the mother's interpreting the infant's signals. It may well be the case that an infant's signals are idiosyncratic and therefore only the mother or other familiar adults may fully understand their meaning. Bower (1977) suggested that this may be the basis of the infant's rejection of strangers in that the stranger may be neither able to interpret the infant's signals nor respond, from the infant's point of view, appropriately. However, Trevarthen (1975, 1977, 1979b), after analysing films of interaction between mothers and their newborn babies, argued that infants as young as 3 weeks would exhibit some intention to communicate and have 'conversations' with their mothers in which they would take turns and 'speak' by mouth movements and hand-waving. His conclusion was:

Analysis of filmed exchanges reveals that while the pattern of communication between mother and infant is regulated by *both* partners, it is indeed one sided and the infant tends to assume control in the course of communication after mother and baby become mutually orientated. I consider the finding that a two-month-old baby may take purposeful initiative in communication as important as the discovery of an innate form of intention to speak with an accompanying code or gesture. . . . The communicative processes of infants are not merely latent precursors of language; they are already functional in directing communication with adults. Thus infants control the social stimulation on which their own development depends. (Trevarthen, 1979b, p. 343)

Since even deaf infants babble and generally infants produce sounds they are not hearing in the language around them (Preston and Yeni-Komshian, 1967), some early pre-speech behaviours are the result of maturation and are not primarily socially elicited. Nevertheless, once they have appeared they can be inhibited or facilitated by social interaction. This was shown by the classic study of Rheingold *et al.* (1959) which showed that the rate of babbling would increase when the infants' sounds were responded to by an adult stroking their stomachs. However, the reason for this increase is not clear. The infants may have been attempting to communicate, or they may have enjoyed affecting the behaviour of the adults by eliciting a response, or they may simply have enjoyed having their stomachs stroked and babbled more to gain that reward. Dodd (1972) showed that babbling would increase in infants aged between 9 and 12 months if vocal and social stimulation by the parents were combined. However, the infants did not imitate their parents directly, in that they did not copy the sounds the parents were making; rather, they quantitatively increased the production of their own sounds. Tonkova-Yampol'skaya (1968) argued that speech begins in intonation, i.e. the pattern of stress and pauses in language, and that with infants under 6 months adults used the infants' intonation to interpret their cries. Intonation develops further in Dore's (1974) second *presyntactic* stage when the infant will use one word to convey several meanings or to stand for a whole sentence (see p. 59). At this stage infants were found (Menyuk and Bernholtz, 1969) to be able to produce single words with the intonational patterns of statements, questions and emphatics. At the third stage of *syntactic communication* words are combined to express meaning, and finally, as infancy ends, cognitive meaning and mode of expression come together and *verbal language* develops.

Studies of infant 'language' differ, at least in emphasis, concerning the nature of the phenomenon. While the course of development – from cries and coos, though single sounds and discrete intonational patterns, to single words and ultimately to sentences – is clearly mapped, the significance of such behaviour, and the factors which instigate and facilitate its development, can be differentially interpreted. Some theorists link language to sensori-motor intelligence; others see it as parasitic upon meaning, i.e. as the means whereby infants express the meanings which they wish to convey; while a third group stresses the social context in which it originates.

Sensori-motor intelligence is often seen as being dominated by perception and rooted in action. It is not reflective in the sense of being able to represent the external internally by means of symbols and reflect upon these symbols in the absence of their referents. Thus Inhelder refers to Piaget as starting from Goethe's proposition 'In the beginning was the deed' (Inhelder, 1962, p. 21), and Piaget does indeed see intelligence, first, as the intentional elaboration of action in the fourth stage of the sensori-motor period and, secondly, as the internalization of such actions into the 'operations' of thought (see p. 106). Thus for him language can only develop at the end of this period, when internal representation and evocative memory begins (see p. 48).

Vygotsky (1962) too believed that action precedes words: 'The word was not the beginning – action was there first; it is the end of development, crowning the deed!' (p. 153). He saw infancy as having 'pre-intellectual' speech, such as babbling, and 'pre-linguistic' thought, i.e. the perceptually dominated action patterns of practical intelligence. When these two come together at the end of infancy, thought becomes verbal and speech rational.

Infant language has been studied mainly by the detailed analysis of the output of single children or small groups of children. While studies of production are more common than studies of comprehension, some of the latter do exist (Edwards, 1978; Barrett, 1978). On the basis of this type of data some support has been found for linking early language with sensori-motor intelligence. Ervin-Tripp (1966) found that the first nouns used seemed to refer to objects with characteristic sizes and visual contours, and the first verbs marked either human or animal movement. Bloom (1970) found infants would use mental-process verbs such as 'look, read, see, show, want and watch', but all were perceptual and, except for 'want', visual. Halliday (1970) also found that infants were able to use verbs expressing reactions and perceptions, such as 'like', 'please', 'see' and 'look', but not verbs expressing cognitions or verbalizations, such as 'think', 'know', 'say' or 'speak'.

Clark (1973) suggested that where infant word meanings do not match adult meaning, in being either too wide or too narrow, what determines infants' usage may be their perceptual abilities. Similarly Nelson (1973) found that infants' earliest words were personal and related mainly to their own actions, rather than being names of things which simply formed part of their environment. When speaking of the first fifty words learned by a group of infants in their second year, she said:

It is apparent that children learn the names of things they can act on . . . as well as things that act themselves such as dogs and cars. They do not learn the names of things in the house or outside that are simply 'there'. . . . With very few exceptions all the words listed are terms applying to manipulable or movable objects. (Nelson, 1973, p. 31)

If language-learning is rooted in sensori-motor intelligence, and if sensori-motor intelligence has a longer evolutionary history than later intelligence and is therefore less variable, then one would expect the process of early language-learning to show a similar uniformity amongst all members of the human species. Slobin (1970), having carried out cross-cultural studies of language-acquisition, has argued that this process in its early stages is the same in all languages, although the languages actually learnt may be very different. Ervin-Tripp (1973) supported this by pointing out the similarity in two lists of early words used by children, the first of which was drawn from Luo children in Kenya (Blount, 1969) and the second from Samoan children (Kernan, 1969). Chomsky (1965) and McNeill (1970a, 1970b) account for this apparent universality of process by positing an innate language-acquisition device (LAD). This device contains, as it were, a template of hypothesized linguistic universals such as 'subject', 'object', 'verb', which infants can apply to the language they are hearing and thus abstract the relevant features to construct their own grammatical competence. In this theory the onus is very much on the infant, who is seen as being born with the equipment to pay selective attention to certain aspects of the language he or she is hearing. Lenneberg (1964, 1967) links this closely to Piaget by saying that language is biologically based and is specific to our species. Thus we speak as we do (Lenneberg) and think as we do (Piaget) because we have a species-specific form of biologically determined organization resulting from evolutionary adaptation.

Those who see language as parasitic upon meaning argue that the infant begins by having a meaning to express, or by picking up the meanings of others non-verbally, and only subsequently learns *how* to express such meanings via verbal language. Thus Halliday (1975a) argued: 'From the functional point of view, as soon as there are meaningful expressions there is language . . . the child has a linguistic system before he has any words or structures at all' (p. 247). MacNamara (1972) was equally direct: 'infants learn their language by first determining, independently of language, the meaning which a speaker intends to convey to them, and by their working out the relationship between the meaning and their language . . . the infant uses meaning as a clue to language, rather than language as a clue to meaning' (p. 1).

Support for this view comes from experiments in imitation

(Fraser *et al.*, 1963; Ervin, 1964), which suggest that while infants do pay attention to aspects of the language they hear around them, such attention is selective in that they will only adapt their linguistic forms of output to make them more like a model's if the model's utterance seems to the infant to be a better way of expressing their meaning. Similarly, when Smith (1970) studied comprehension she found that older infants, of 2 years, were able to understand the meanings of sentences in syntactic forms which they could not produce, but that the younger infants responded more readily to commands that were expressed in their own shortened form of language. Thus, at least at the end of the sensori-motor period, language-production seems to lag behind comprehension. Bowerman (1973) argued that an understanding of semantic relations would precede the ability to express such an understanding grammatically. She too noted that children first name 'objects acted upon', and claimed that the reason was that this was a semantic category, whereas 'all objects' was a syntactic category and thus if the semantic category and the syntactic category had been equivalent the infant should have learned both at the same time. Brown (1973), having conducted a cross-cultural study, found that the majority of first-word utterances amongst twelve unacquainted children speaking four different languages could be grouped into a short list of semantic relations:

1. Agent and action
2. Action and object
3. Agent and object
4. Action and locative or location
5. Entity and locative or location
6. Possessor and possession
7. Entity and attributive
8. Demonstrative and entity (Brown, 1973, p. 173)

In one sense it seems obvious that, since language is not without content, the understanding of content must precede the expression of it. However, to emphasize meaning is also to emphasize the communicative function of language, for meaning is, by definition, interpersonal in that to exist it requires both to be expressed and to be understood. Thus, for Bruner (1978) language has its origins in the need for joint reference and in the joint action of mother and child, in particular by their jointly attending to a single object. He holds that children 'communicate' before they have language. Interestingly, he combines the notions of language being rooted in action and of semantics preceding syntax by arguing that what must be understood in order for the child to understand action, and hence be able to engage in joint action, parallels the structure of speech development: that is 'knowing what is done to what, by whom, to whom, where, by what instrument and in what order' (p. 67), requires that subjects, objects, locations, etc., be marked and this is what the young child first attends to.

Bates et al. (1977) have shown that the development of communication is affected more by infants developing a notion of means–end behaviour, or basic causality, than it is by the development of 'static' cognitive schemes such as that of object permanence. Such an understanding of causality could cause the infant to seek a particular type of joint action, namely to seek for adult help, and this may further language development in the way Bruner suggested.

As Redshaw and Hughes (1975) pointed out, gorilla infants, although ahead of human infants on most sensori-motor tasks, neither use tools nor seek help in a task. They suggest that: 'It may be that the failure to produce language-like systems in higher primates is due to the failure to produce certain kinds of means–end analysis that permit communication to develop' (p. 286).

Halliday (1975b) stresses that language is a social phenomenon and describes the development of infant language in terms of the functions it serves for the child. All his data come from the intensive study of one child, Nigel, although there has been some independent support for his findings (Carter, 1974; Dore, 1975). From 10½ months to 16 months Nigel used sounds in four ways: to express his needs and wants (instrumental); to effect the behaviour of others (regulatory); to interact with others (interpersonal); and to express his awareness of himself (personal). The next stage showed a rapid increase in vocabulary, the start of some grammar and the emergence of two new functions, the 'learning or mathetic function', as exemplified by 'What's that?' questions, and a 'pragmatic' function which seeks to control events rather than understand them. At this stage Nigel used intonation to distinguish between these two functions, using a rising tone for the pragmatic and a falling one for the mathetic. At 18 months dialogue began with his being able to ask 'What's that?' and the social role of language began to be fully established. Once the child can use language to learn about the world he or she has gone beyond sensori-motor intelligence, since language use presupposes the ability to realize that a sign, i.e. a word, can stand for its referent. Thus when children ask 'What's that?', meaning 'What is it called?', they have moved beyond sensori-motor intelligence which limited the infant to acting directly upon the environment. Now they can observe it and comment upon its attributes in the company of another via a verbal mode of exchange of meanings.

Individual differences

Sensori-motor intelligence may well be a highly adaptive form of intelligence which we share with other species besides our own and which will be, potentially, similar for all humans. While different environments may lead to the actualization of more or less of this potential, nevertheless less individual variability is to be expected. Provided a child is exposed to a normal human environment all children can be expected to attain the same level of functioning at the end of this period, i.e. no normal child will remain at the level of sensori-motor intelligence, nor will any normal child fail to progress through this stage in a similar manner to others. Individual differences can be found between infants but these are differences in degree rather than in kind. Two questions of interest are, first, given the overall similarity between infants, what do these differences consist in? And, secondly, is there any evidence that measures of infant functioning are predictive of later functioning?

There have been some attempts to assess infant intelligence and development in general by means of standardized 'tests'. Some of the earliest, but still in use, are the Bayley infant scales of mental and motor development (Bayley, 1933a, 1933b, 1935). Equally well known are Cattell's infant intelligence scale (1940), the Griffiths scale (1954) and the Gersell schedules (Gersell and Amatruda, 1941), devised as part of the longitudinal Berkeley growth study. More recently tests limited to specific types of behaviour have become more popular as Uzgiris and Hunt's (1966) test of sensori-motor skills.

Testing is of value when assessing infants thought to be

defective in some way in that, if a 'norm' can be arrived at, gross deviations from such a norm may need further investigation; and testing may be of value in research studies of factors thought to affect infant functioning. However, any discussion of differences between infants is better viewed primarily as a description of functioning rather than as an evaluation of that functioning as 'better' or 'worse'. In any case, studies of differences between individuals within groups are likely to be of more value to those interested in the course of cognitive growth than are studies of differences between cultures or large sub-cultural groups. Given the number of variables that need to be considered in the cross-cultural studies, it is difficult to see how an investigation can possibly extract the relevant factors, and their relative weightings, when trying to account for the test scores arrived at by individuals in the large groups being compared: the differences between individuals within a group (within-group variance) can turn out to be as significant as the overall, averaged difference between the groups (between-group variance). While such large-scale cross-cultural studies may provide the data for many statistically based arguments, at present they add little to our understanding of development and the factors which affect it.

Some within-group studies have pointed to factors which may affect cognitive development at least during infancy. These can be broadly divided into those which concentrate on differences between infants and those that stress differences between infants' environments. Infants may be born more or less responsive to their surroundings. Birns (1965) showed that within their first five days different infants would show a 'strong', 'moderate' or 'mild' response to stimuli which was consistent irrespective of the stimuli used (in her study these consisted of soft and loud tones, a dummy put into the infants' mouths and a cold disc put on their thighs). Some appear more able to control the level of stimuli they receive than others. Murphy and Moriarty (1976) found that some were successful in filtering out too intense stimuli, whereas others were not. However this depended, to an extent, on their particular area of sensitivity since visual stimuli could be controlled by either looking away or shutting their eyes whereas auditory stimulation could not be sought or inhibited in a similar way. The infants' initial response may affect the way in which adults interact with them and hence affect their subsequent development; for an alert, reasonably active infant is likely to be more rewarding to the care-giver and hence get more attention than one who is either over-active and tense or unresponsive and dull (Bennett, 1971).

A particularly important infant characteristic is motivation to learn. This may be partly inborn but will also be influenced by the infant's environment. Papoušek and Papoušek (1967, 1969, 1975) showed that infants were born with a tendency to seek solutions to problems for the sheer joy of doing so. In their studies they tested infants aged 3 days, 3 months and 5 months and found that the infants would learn a sequence of head moves simply to bring on a display of lights but soon lost interest if the experimenter repeatedly switched them off and on. They would also continue to learn sequences of moves even when they did not wish to have the 'reward' of a drink of milk. Solving the problems seemed sufficient to make the infants smile and relax. However, if the task was too difficult the infants who 'failed' would withdraw and then try to avoid anything connected with the task. Obviously infants will seek both to explore and affect their environment. Depending on the results of their endeavours, this initial motivation will either develop further or be inhibited, and the child will develop a hopeful or hopeless orientation towards affecting the environment (Turner, 1980).

Several studies have concentrated on the environment in which the infant and young child is reared. That of Yarrow *et al.* (1975), covering the first six months, was based on observations of the children in their homes, and concentrated on both the infants' social environment and the inanimate objects available to them. They tested the infants by using (i) the Bayley scales, (ii) some items to measure problem-solving, (iii) a test of exploratory behaviour and (iv) a test of preference for novel stimuli. They observed the way in which the infants were directly stimulated by people; the variety, complexity and feedback potential of the inanimate objects available in their environments; and what they called the 'social mediation of inanimate objects', i.e. 'the ways in which the caregiver directed the infants' attention to play materials or highlighted their properties' (Yarrow *et al.*, 1975, p. 19). The advantage of this study was that it was able to point to correlations between specific features of the environment and specific features of infant behaviour. Since a correlation does not imply a causal connection, their findings should not be taken as suggesting a picture of cause and effect but rather as pointing to suggestive relationships between variables. First, they considered whether the stimulation of specific modalities would selectively affect infant development and found that this was the case. Kinesthetic stimulation was particularly important perhaps because it enabled the infants to define the boundaries of their own bodies and hence distinguish themselves from the environment in general. Secondly, maternal responsiveness and the way in which the mother expressed positive feelings were found to have specific effects: a mother who responded to her infant's coos and babbling caused an increased output of these, whereas prompt response to crying had a more general effect and seemed to lead to an infant who was more highly motivated to pursue tasks. If the mother drew the infant's attention to toys but showed little further interaction, the infant was found to seek and play with objects more than those who did not have their attention drawn to them. If the mother talked and smiled at the infant at the same time as pointing to objects then the result was an increase in vocalization by the infant, not an increase in exploration. 'Talking' seemed more important than exploring the object *per se*. With respect to the inanimate environment, once again specific aspects of the objects available had specific effects on the infant (p. 97). 'Responsiveness' or feedback was particularly salient. The authors' explanation of this is:

> The responsive qualities of toys reinforce the infant's efforts at manipulating objects and this activity in turn helps to improve his fine motor-skills. The development of prehensile skills enables the infant to elicit more feedback from objects, further reinforcing his efforts to master the environment. (Yarrow *et al.*, 1975, p. 98)

They conclude that the stimulation the infant receives from people has a quite different effect from that stemming from inanimate objects and that the two environments are not interchangeable. Furthermore, within each of these environments specific features had specific effects which were enhanced or diminished by the individual characteristics of the infants. Detailed studies of this kind, even with small samples, are particularly valuable in attempting to link discrete areas of infant development with specifiable aspects of infants' environments.

White *et al.* (1979) combined their observations of infants' environments with a training programme. (The latter will be considered below; see p. 41.) First, they observed infants in their homes as part of a longitudinal study. They found that infants who were developing well were characterized particularly by having four forms of experience: first, they had adults who would act as a resource and thus enable them to learn how to 'procure the service of another'; secondly, they learned how to gain the attention of adults without being attention-seeking; thirdly, they spent time gaining information by 'steadily staring at objects' rather than just looking quickly at them; and finally, they had live language directed towards them, as opposed to overhearing others talking or listening to the radio or television. Children who were developing less well, on the other hand, were found to have more restrictions placed on their movements by being placed in play-pens, for example. They also spent more time than did the others 'passing time', or being bored, and engaging in gross motor activities such as climbing on and off objects and trying to get objects. Good care-givers were characterized by arranging their homes in such a way that their children had the maximum opportunity to crawl or walk round and explore without doing damage to themselves or the home; by being available as a 'consultant' to the child when needed to provide assistance or reassurance, but not interfering with the child's activities; and by setting clear limits in disciplining the child but using procedures which were appropriate for the infant's age. These were distraction for children below 1 year, distraction and/or separation of the child from the object between 12 and 18 months, and these procedures plus 'firm verbal restrictions' over 18 months.

Carew (1980) carried out a related study which aimed to explore a series of significant distinctions. First, the distinction between 'intellectually profitable' interactions between infants and care-givers and other interactions; and secondly, the roles played by each, i.e. the extent to which the child or the care-giver was, separately, the primary source of the intellectual experience or whether it occurred in a reciprocal situation with both sides creating it. In her study Carew collected longitudinal and observational data on young children's experiences in the home and in a day-care centre to see which of these correlated with IQ, as assessed on the Binet scale, at age 3. Her sample was small, consisting of twenty-three home-based and twenty-three day-care infants, but nevertheless her findings are suggestive. It proved possible to distinguish between the 'intellectual experiences' of language-mastery, spatial, perceptual and fine-motor mastery, concrete reasoning and expressive-artistic skill mastery, and 'other experiences' such as play, exploration, basic care, routine talk, etc. Only the former were predictive of test performance at age 3. Those experiences which related to language-mastery were the most significant before 2½ years of age; after this the role of the care-giver in structuring the child's environment so as to give experiences in the other three areas was highly predictive of later IQ. The children's scores at 3 were only positively affected overall when an interacting adult was the sole or a joint source of the child's experience. Solitary intellectual experiences did not have the same effect. In the home-based group solitary play after 2½ was predictive of later IQ, but this finding did not occur in the day-care group. In the final analysis, 55 per cent of the child's IQ variance was attributable to the care-giver being the source of the intellectual experience and only 15 per cent to the child as the sole source. In sum, Carew's work showed that a child's IQ will be correlated with certain types of prior experience particularly those related to language. Her findings are correlational and therefore do not imply cause and effect, but she does ask several important questions and attempts to disentangle various forms of environmental influence.

In general it is really not possible to look at 'overall development'. What needs to be looked at is the significance of specific experiences in specific environments leading to specific outcomes.

Intervention programmes

An outcome of studies which point to the effect of environmental variables on infant cognitive development has been the instigation of a number of 'intervention programmes' designed to help parents provide the kind of environment for their children which, it is hoped, will facilitate their cognitive growth. For example White *et al.* (1979) tested the finding of their observational project experimentally. They divided the families in their sample into an experimental group which they visited regularly, giving advice on child-rearing in accordance with the findings of their observational project, and control groups. One control group received advice and visits from an experienced and eminent pediatrician, one was visited and tested but given no guidance, and one was just seen and tested at the beginning and end of the project. They found that the behaviour of the parents in both the experimental and control groups was significantly different towards their first-born children and towards later-born children and that this difference overrode the difference between the conditions. When first-borns alone were considered all the children appeared to be developing well, with the experimental group doing slightly better. The later-borns did not seem to benefit and the authors suggest that 'the simplest explanation for this result is that the child rearing practices of first time parents are more sensitive to change than those of parents of two or more children' (White *et al.*, 1979, p. 123).

As a result of this project the research team set up their Centre for Parent Education which plans to educate parents and potential parents as well as running courses for professionals who are engaged in helping families with young children. Similar to this was the Florida parent education programme (Gordon and Guinagh, 1974; Guinagh and Gordon, 1976), based on Piagetian concepts, which used specially trained women from the local community to act as parent educators. The children of the project were followed up for ten years. It was found that continuous intervention lasting two to three years in the first three years of life affected the children's intellectual level and achievement in the junior school, but no differences in motivation or adjustment to school were found between the children who had taken part in the project and a matched group who had not.

There have been a number of such programmes over the past few years (reviewed by Beller, 1979). Virtually all of them had short-term effects in that children in the programmes appeared to be developing better than matched groups who were not receiving such attention. The long-term effects require a more complex method of analysis. Some studies quoted by Beller have found beneficial effects of intervention on subsequent performance. However, infant IQ in itself has not, generally, been found to be highly predictive of later IQ (Bayley, 1940; Honzig *et al.*, 1948; Brown and Halpern, 1971; Lewis and McGurk, 1972). This finding could be predicted if Scarr-Salapatek (1976) is correct in her view that infant intelligence is different in kind from later intelligence in that it has a long evolutionary history and therefore shows less individual variation than the phylogenetically more recent later intelligence. Beller (1974) found that 'autonomous achievement striving' was strongly predictive of later academic performance. He suggested that the intervention programmes may be having long-term effects on infants' attitudes which, in turn, lead to intellectual achievement. However, many of the parent educators are striving to enable the parents to instil specific skills. He argued that an emphasis on skill in infant education programmes is occurring at the moment when primary and secondary schools, at least in the United States, are turning away from such a traditional approach towards more discovery-based learning, which stresses intrinsic motivation, with the result that 'disadvantaged lower-class infants and pre-schoolers are being made to catch up with what middle-class elementary schools and high schools are turning away from' (Beller, 1974, p. 891).

Conclusion

Infancy undoubtedly marks the start of a person's cognitive development. The newborn is adapted to pay selective attention to relevant stimuli, to solve problems and to interact socially. While infant performance will be affected by specific features of both the social and non-social environments, provided that these environments are normally stimulating, development should in the sensori-motor period proceed normally and similarly for all non-handicapped infants. Intervention programmes appear to do no harm and may be beneficial, at least for first-borns. However, being in relationship with other humans may be more significant for healthy growth. White et al. (1979) point out the limits of intervention by saying: 'Parent educators can do very little for families with the greatest needs. Families with multiple stresses such as serious health, employment and economic needs are, in our opinion, beyond the capacity of educators' (p. 182). This may well be true, and the implication appears to be that scarce resources should be allocated in such a way that families will be more able to nurture their own children's early cognitive growth by loving and stimulating interaction in an environment which provides at least the minimal material requirements for family life.

3

The pre-school years (2–5)

By the age of 2 the child has, with the development of language and the ability to conceptualize action sequences, moved out of the perceptually dominated world of infancy. During the years before starting school at the age of 5 children's cognition is characterized by being in the stage Piaget described as 'pre-operational' and by the development of the ability to represent the external world to themselves and to communicate their understanding to others by means of symbolic systems such as language.

Pre-operational intelligence

During early childhood the practical intelligence of the sensori-motor period is transformed into 'operational' intelligence, or the internalization of the earlier overt actions (see p. 49). Between the ending of the sensori-motor period, at 18 months to 2 years, and the start of operational thinking, at approximately 7 years, the child is in the transitional stage of preparation for operations. The form of intelligence which characterizes this stage is the ground from which true operational intelligence develops. It should not be seen negatively, as a period when the child 'fails' to employ adult logic, but rather as a stage in which the child's thinking has distinct characteristics, which are indeed different in kind from those of adults but which represent the best form of adaptation that children can make in the process of constructing their understanding of reality. Thus the apparent mistakes, or logical lapses, of this period reflect the child's attempts to grapple with reality, though which mature thinking will develop.

First, pre-operational children, sensibly enough, start from where they are and to a greater or lesser extent distort reality as they attempt to assimilate it, or make sense of it, using the cognitive schemes, or ways of understanding, which they have developed. Thus children's thinking is, when compared with that of adults, centred on the self, or *egocentric*, to a greater extent and in more situations. However, it is not wholly egocentric, nor is the adult's free of egocentrism. By 'egocentrism' Piaget meant that the young child centred on his or her own point of view or perspective and did not realize that others had different points of view. His famous three-mountain-problem is often used to illustrate this (Piaget and Inhelder, 1948/1956). The child is seated before a model of three mountains which differ in colour, size and location. A doll is then placed either opposite or at right angles to the child, so that the doll and the child are at different angles to the model. The child is then asked to choose a photograph which would correspond to the doll's perspective or to rearrange the mountain so as to reconstruct the doll's view. Pre-operational children were found not to be able to carry out this task. However, the three-mountain-task is complex for it requires children not just to realize that the doll will have a different perspective but also what that perspective is and, having deduced the doll's perspective, to be able to reproduce it correctly. If children are given a much simpler task, in which, say, they are shown a rectangular block which has a picture of a teddy bear on one side and a duck on the other, with the ends, top and bottom blank, and they realize that when they can see the teddy the doll can see the duck and vice versa, what are we justified in concluding about their cognitive powers? Chandler and Boyes (1982) argue that in a simple task young children are well aware of who can see what, i.e. that the doll can see the duck, but what they are thinking about is the block

45

and its properties, namely a teddy on one side and a duck on the other. Thus they are not thinking about the doll's perspective at all, that is they do not realize that knowledge can be subjectively organized.

> Knowledge for such pre-operational subjects seems to reside entirely within the world of material objects and, as such, is a feature of things rather than of persons and is thus given like a present to all those who are in a position to receive it. (Chandler and Boyes, 1982, p. 392)

Thus if children know what is on the other side of the block they will also know what anyone in line with that side will see. The initial step is for young children to realize that the model or object has *two sides*, that is they have to realize first something about the object. Flavell *et al.* (1981) showed that though children failed to realize that a turtle that appeared right-way up to one person would be upside down to another viewing it at an angle of 180 degrees to the first, nevertheless succeeded in understanding that some people would see the turtle's feet and others its back once a screen was placed in such a position as to divide the turtle down the centre. Gradually the child will realize that what other people see is not, necessarily, what he or she sees; that is what other people see, while being related to the properties of the objects seen, is essentially a construction of the perceiver. It will therefore differ from that of the self both because the other has a different view of the object and because the other will subjectively organize that view.

Thus, if children are to move from thinking that their point of view is the only one, they have to learn, first, the properties of objects, secondly, that others have a different perspective and thirdly what that perspective is. This ability is called '*role-taking*' and its development in children has been studied in many contexts so that one can speak of 'social', 'affective', 'spatial' or 'cognitive' role-taking. Light (1979) studied the role-taking abilities of children aged $4\frac{1}{2}$. He found differences in ability between the children which, he claimed, could be related to different kinds of social experience within the family, in particular their mode of interaction with their mothers. Interestingly, reading ability at $6\frac{1}{2}$ was found to be more highly correlated with role-taking ability at $4\frac{1}{2}$ than it was with IQ at that age. Obviously the ability to realize

46

both that other minds have points of view and that these do not necessarily coincide with one's own is a fairly sophisticated piece of cognition. It is one which seems to be fostered by mothers who consciously take account of the fact that the child's view is important and treat them in a 'personal' way. Thus, for example, discipline is dealt with by bargaining, or by concessions of the kind 'Do it when you've finished', rather than by a show of physical force or statement of authority such as 'You do it now because I told you to!' Clearly if the child's view is not attended to, a realization that it exists will be impeded.

The egocentrism of pre-operational children is but one manifestation of a more pervasive aspect of their thinking which is their tendency to centre on one aspect of a situation or salient feature of a display and fail to take other, equally relevant, aspects into account. Thus they will concentrate on states, especially final states, without considering the transformations by means of which the states were achieved. This failure to de-centre and to consider transformations is what gives pre-operational thinking its fluid character, in that children do not see that a previous state has any necessary connection with a later one. For example, if children are shown a static display of ten counters in one-to-one correspondence with ten sweets and agree that the number of counters is the same as the number of sweets, they will not 'conserve' this numerical equivalence if either of the rows is transformed in such a way as to destroy the perceptual one-to-one correspondence. These children divorce the pre-transformational state from the post-transformational one and do not understand that, if the numbers or counters and sweets were equivalent before, they will be equivalent after unless there have been some material additions or subtractions. Piaget (1964/1980) described this characteristic as follows:

> The child perceives by means of simple one way actions with centration on the *states* (and, above all, on the *final* states) without the decentration which alone permits the conceptualisation of 'transformations' as such. The basic consequence is that the conservation of objects, sets, quantities etc. is not immediate before operational decentration is achieved. (p. 79)

This failure to consider transformations gives pre-operational thinking its third defining characteristic, namely its *irreversibility*.

47

The young child does not appear to realize that certain transformations can be reversed so that material in its end state can be returned to its initial state by reversing the transformation. If 2 plus 2 equals 4, then 4 minus 2 *must* equal 2. A concentration on states can lead the child, according to Piaget, to believe in the case of a reversal, that there are *two* changes, one between the initial and the end state, and one between the end and the initial state, which restores the status quo. For example, the amount of plasticine in two balls X and Y may be agreed to be equal in initial state *a* when $X = Y$; to be unequal in state *b* when one ball has been reshaped into a sausage or pancake, so that $X = Y^1$, and then, once again to be equal in state *c* when the manipulated ball of plasticine is rolled back into a ball again, so that now $X = Y^2$.

There are however some cognitive achievements peculiar to the pre-operational stage. At this stage the child develops the notion of invariance with respect to qualitative identity and to 'functions'. Thus the child who thinks that the *amount* of plasticine in a ball may change after the ball has been reshaped is capable of understanding that it is, nevertheless, the 'same' plasticine – i.e. the child conservers *qualitative*, but not *quantitative* identity. In one study (Piaget *et al.*, 1968, quoted by Flavell, 1977) when a piece of wire was twisted and then straightened again, 3-year-old children seemed to ignore the changes and said it was the same wire; 4-year-olds noticed the changes and denied it was the same wire; and 5-year-olds, while maintaining that it was the same wire, denied that it was the same length when twisted.

By 'functions' Piaget meant the relationship between two entities A and B such that B is dependent in certain respects on A. There would be a functional relationship between a rise or fall in temperature (A) and the length of the mercury in the tube of a thermometer (B). What the young child realizes is that B is affected by A but not to what extent this is so, and therefore, once again, the child's understanding is qualitative rather than quantitative.

The growth of representational skills

Piaget's theory of the development of the semiotic function

Piaget and Inhelder (1966b/1969) used the term 'semiotic function' to refer to the ways in which people represent to themselves both the outside world and their own actions and experiences. This ability to make one thing stand for another goes beyond sensori-motor intelligence. It encompasses more than language, for it includes imitation, symbolic play, drawing, mental images and memory. It was thought to start between 18 months and 2 years, when the child begins to be able to represent actions internally and both anticipate and reflect upon events. Children's thought becomes more wide ranging through the use of the semiotic function than when it was limited to action and perception requiring immediate contact with objects. At the same time the semiotic function is influenced by children's developing intelligence.

Piaget considered these functions in four books – *The Language and Thought of the Child* (1923/1926), *Play, Dreams and Imitation in Childhood* (1946/1951), *Memory and Intelligence* (Piaget and Inhelder, 1968/1973) and *The Mental Imagery of the Child* (Piaget and Inhelder, 1966a). A good summary of his ideas can be found in Piaget and Inhelder's *The Psychology of the Child* (1966b/1969). He saw imitation as marking the transition between the sensori-motor period and representative behaviour proper. He argued that, initially, there is merely reflex contagion, similar to adult yawning, followed shortly by 'sporadic imitation' when infants will copy a sound or movement if it is one which they have in their repertoire of behaviours. This gives way to more systematic imitation, but infants are not able to produce this at will in the presence of adult models. Finally movements which have been seen in others but not in the self, such as tongue movements, can be copied. The next phase shows the move from imitation to intelligence. At first children can copy a model's action with objects, such as turning a door handle, but not for the reasons that the model performs the action, i.e. opening the door. Once children do imitate action to attain a goal Piaget sees the behaviour as intelligent, since they have now 'accommodated' their schemes to the requirements of the object, i.e. they have learned how to turn a handle – not just for the joy of so doing, which is what motivated imitation. At the end of this period children will be able to imitate the model in the latter's absence since the actions have now become internalized and part of their own repertoire by the use of internal symbols or signs.

Piaget distinguished three types of play: games with rules, exercise games, which consisted of physical actions performed simply for the pleasure of exercising a particular skill, and symbolic play. The latter was thought to start at about the age of 2 and be at its height at 5. In symbolic play children seek to re-live events, not just to remember them, and, more importantly, to 'assimilate reality to the self'. That is the pleasure in such play resides in the fact that the child can change the real world, internally, into the wished-for world and become any person he or she wishes, able to perform any action, to bring about anything desired. For Piaget it represented a pure form of egocentric thinking which was more marked only in dreams and day-dreams. It was, however, a true activity of thought since the child had to create, imaginatively, this desired world.

Drawing was seen, by Piaget, as being half-way between the egocentric symbolic play and true mental images. It shares with play the fact that it is done purely for its own sake and exclusively represents the child's point of view, being centred on the self. However it also attempts, even if unsuccessfully, to represent the real world and is in this more like a true mental image. Children's drawings have been found by researchers in all cultures to pass through a similar series of states (Kellogg, 1969). At first they are merely scribbles, possibly signifying no more than another form of action with no representational features. During the pre-school period children begin to match their drawings to real objects (Gombrich, 1960). Here it appears that having 'made' a drawing they then recognize a similarity between it and a real-world object. They then intentionally begin to produce drawings which represent objects in their world, and their drawings become truly symbolic. However, while they are able to produce symbolic representations of reality, not until the age of 7 or 8 are they able to reproduce what they actually see rather than what they know to be there. They will draw two eyes when copying the profile of a face, or draw a cup with a handle although the model cup before them has been positioned so that the handle is in fact hidden (Freeman and Janikoun, 1972).

Representation of the real world in images was not thought to be merely a copy of the world, but rather a construction based on the person's action schemes. Therefore Piaget saw mental images as developing fairly late, since they are not based purely on perception, as theorists who hold images to be copies of reality believe, but on internalized imitation. Piaget distinguished be-

50

tween the mainly static 'reproductive images', which he thought characterized the child's images before the ages of 7 or 8, and 'kinetic' images of changes in state, which occurred after that age. In his discussion of this we can see how the development of the semiotic function is intertwined with the child's level of adaptive intelligence, or 'operatory' understanding. Before the age of 7 or 8, Piaget argued, children cannot imagine stages in transformations between states, as when a stick moves from the vertical to the horizontal, since they do not understand the process of such movements. Only when the *process* is understood will they be able to represent that process internally and therefore develop anticipatory images which can then, in turn, further the development of thinking by allowing them to consider states and changes of state internally. Mental images mark the culmination of the construction during the semiotic period of a coherent system of internal representation.

A considerable amount of discussion concerning the role played by imagery in thought has gone beyond Piaget. It concerns what an image is and what it does; or whether visual aids, once internalized, are either visual or aids. It has been argued that a mental image is like an internal picture and is thus an object of *visual* perception and memory, as opposed to verbal memory and abstract or 'propositional' storage. Supporters of this view have shown that a person's memory for visual images is impaired if they have to carry out a visual-perception task at the same time (Atwood, 1971; Salthouse, 1974). Baddeley *et al.* (1975) demonstrated that a visual-tracking task interfered with the memory of a spatial array which required a visual image, but not with the memory of verbal nonsense syllables which did not. However, the same task was found to affect memory of concrete noun/adjective verbal pairs (which could be imaged) and abstract pairs (which could not be imaged). Some argue that information is stored as abstract propositions (Anderson and Bower, 1973) but that visual inputs contain more material and hence are 'richer' than the 'leaner', more abstract verbal inputs. Paivio (1969) posited the existence of two systems, i.e. verbal and visual memory, which has received support from studies of brain-damaged patients. Damage to the left hemisphere seems to impair verbal recognition and damage to the right hemisphere visual recognition, as in the case of the Japanese patient who, with a damaged left hemisphere, could no longer read the Kana language, which has phonetic characters, but could read the Kanji syllabary, which has ideographic, picture-like, characters (Sasanuma, 1974). Normal people presumably use both systems in parallel in such a way that, although the verbal may take precedence, the visual will facilitate recognition and retrieval.

Imagery could be seen to aid thought in that it presents information simultaneously whereas verbal information is, necessarily, sequential. Thus the ability to consider all aspects of a spatial array will be facilitated by visual rather than verbal storage. Miller (1975) found that sighted children, who had been blindfolded and learned a spatial array by touch, were able to recall positions in both reverse and forward order since they had translated their haptic (touch-and-movement) imagery into spatial imagery. Congenitally blind children who were limited to haptic imagery could not use reverse order. However, the development of language seems to enable blind adults to compensate, and their performance on, for example, chess problems is not necessarily less skilled than that of sighted adults.

The development of memory

Piaget considered memory in his discussion of the semiotic function and, in accordance with his emphasis on knowledge as constructed, saw memory as an *active* coding and recoding system, as opposed to a system in which a memory once laid down remains unchanged until the moment of recall. He believed (Piaget and Inhelder, 1968/1973) that memories were reconstructed as the child's operatory understanding developed, so that what was recalled was shaped more by the child's intellectual level at the moment of recall than it was by what was stored when the memory originated. He suggested that during storage a person's memories are reconstructed in accordance with the way the person's own construction of reality develops. Piaget and Inhelder therefore linked the ability to memorize with a person's level of intellectual development. For example, 6-year-olds were shown a glass bottle half filled with liquid and then, when it had been removed, were asked to draw it. The majority did not draw the liquid's level as horizontal, which related to their failure to realize that the level would be horizontal irrespective of the jar's orientation. However, when asked to draw the picture after a lapse of six months some of the children did recall the liquid as being horizontal, despite their previous failure to do so. Similarly children, if shown serially ordered sticks, will fail to serialize on the initial recall but will do so subsequently. Therefore, for Piaget, memory equalled 'applied cognition', as Flavell (1971) argued:

> What we call 'memory processes' seem largely to be just the same old, familiar, cognitive processes but as they are applied to a particular class of problems . . . memory seems . . . to be . . . the head doing its characteristic 'thing' while coping with the specific task of storing or retrieving factual information, ideas, and other cognitive contents. (p. 273)

There have been several attempts to test Piaget's theory but, to date, the results have been inconclusive. Altemeyer *et al.* (1969) showed that not only did memory for serially ordered sticks improve over time, in confirmation of Piaget, but also that if children were shown a non-ordered array of sticks they would, after a time lapse, recall them too as ordered. This indicates that the improvement shown in the Piagetian studies may not reflect intellectual development but be another example of the phenomenon, called 'rationalisation' by Bartlett (1932), whereby when material is recalled after a lapse of time it is 'smoothed' or 'reordered' to make it more regular. Alternatively, as Bayraktar (1979) argued, the apparent improvement in the children's memory for the serialized sticks may be more a function of their ability to draw what they remembered accurately. While Dahlem (1968, 1969) found evidence of improvement after six months, Maurer *et al.* (1979) found that only 15 per cent had improved and, in addition, a number of children were found to have regressed. Kail and Hagen (1982) comment that 'in none of the replication studies has the number of improvements significantly surpassed the number of regressions' (p. 355).

Various models of memory have been proposed which go beyond Piaget's and which are used to organize much current theorizing on memory development. Generally, memory is seen as a set of processes which give rise to a mnemonic response and which consist in ways of taking in, coding, sorting, storing and retrieving information. More specifically, Atkinson and Shriffrin (1968) distinguished structural, biologically determined features

53

of memory from the control process used by an individual. Immediate, short-term and long-term memory formed part of the former whereas the latter covered strategies for remembering such as rehearsal, and it is the development of the latter which may determine the superior memory performance of older children.

Theories of memory and its development have significance for education since, even today, many educational tests which claim to be tests of attainment, for example unseen examinations relating to specific subjects, are covert tests of memory, albeit memory of a certain content. Memory is also involved in much formal learning in the classroom, to the extent that children's so-called 'understanding' may, in fact, reflect little more than their ability, or failure, to memorize. If teachers were to become aware of the characteristics of children's memory they could take this into account in their teaching methods and might indeed devise methods which would improve the development of their pupils' memories.

Myers and Perlmutter (1978) studied memory development in children aged 3 to 5 and found that even the youngest children had good *recognition* memory but that this too improved during the age range studied. In their first study the children were shown eighteen unrelated items which were then hidden. They were then shown thirty-six items, consisting of the eighteen original items and eighteen new ones, and asked to say whether or not each individual item had been in the first group. The 2-year-olds averaged 81 per cent correct recognitions and the 4-year-olds 92 per cent, a statistically significant difference. When the children were asked to *recall* previously seen items the older children performed considerably better than the younger ones. However, both age groups found it easier to recall the last items seen.

Myers and Perlmutter also found that even the youngest children's memory was facilitated by their knowledge about the world, but this was different in kind from the knowledge effects apparent in older children (see p. 97). With the youngest children it seemed that experience-based knowledge gave rise to an *automatic* associative process; as soon as an item was presented to the child it was associatively paired with any relevant knowledge the child had, but this did not involve any intentional strategy to aid memory. These young children were found to remember items more easily if they formed part of a knowledge-based network of association than if they did not or if they violated them. The authors quote a study by Staub (1973) who showed children pairs of pictures: three pairs were pictures of unrelated items; three pairs were of items belonging to the same conceptual category, for example hat and sock; three pairs consisted of one picture showing an item which was part of the item in the other picture, for example tyre and car; and three pairs consisted of one picture representing the habitat of the creature depicted in the other, for example fish and lake. The older children remembered more than the younger, but for all children the part–whole and the habitat relationships were more easily recalled than were those in the same category. All types of related pairs were easier to recall than unrelated pairs. Further evidence that children as young as 3 use some conceptual encoding was given by Faulkender et al. (1974). They showed children aged 2 to 3 unfamiliar pictures, some from the same conceptual category as pictures previously seen and some from unrelated categories. They demonstrated that while the children looked longer at both sets of new pictures, they looked longest at those which were from unfamiliar categories, suggesting that they had used some form of categorical encoding that made those from the same category more 'familiar'. Kail and Hagan (1982) concluded: 'Almost as soon as children can speak well their mnemonic representations of individual pictures and words seem to be semantically based' (p. 375).

However, young children's recognition memory for pictures has been found to differ from that of older children and adults. Children aged 3 to 5 recognize certain pictures of single objects as easily as adults (Brown and Scott, 1971), but realistic pictures were easier for the children to remember than abstracts, and abstracts easier than puzzle pictures (Nelson, 1971). If objects were grouped together into meaningful scenes, or tableaux, after five days the adults remembered the scenes nearly as accurately as the single objects, 9-year-olds exhibited 80 per cent accuracy with scenes as opposed to 90 per cent with single objects and the 6-year-olds only 56 per cent accuracy (Newcombe et al., 1977). If the objects to be remembered are human faces, Carey and Diamond (1977) showed, young children rely on single, individual features, unlike older children and adults who use all the features in their appropriate location to recognize pictures of unfamiliar faces seen once before. Young children behave like adults who have suffered

55

damage to the right posterior cerebral cortex, and therefore Carey and Diamond argued that development of recognition of faces is a function of the development of the right cerebral hemisphere.

Children appear to have a poorer short-term memory capacity than adults. However, Chi (1976, 1977) argued that children's short-term memory may not itself be at fault; rather they do not know how to use appropriate encoding strategies, such a verbal rehearsal, and if adults are prevented from using the appropriate strategies they perform no better than children. It seems that young children do not realize that strategies such as rehearsal do aid recall. Flavell *et al.* (1966) tested children aged 5, 7 and 10. In their study the experimenter showed the children an array of pictures, then pointed to three of them and told the children that, when asked, they had to name the pictures the experimenter had touched in the order he had done so. The interval was fifteen seconds, and during it the visors of the toy space helmets the children were wearing were lowered so that they could not see the pictures. One of the experimenters was able to lip read, and the number of children who used verbal rehearsal, at least in so far as it was demonstrated by their moving their lips, was checked for each age level. While only two of the 5-year-olds were seen to use rehearsal, twelve 7-year-olds and seventeen 10-year-olds did so. Organized rehearsal is more effective than simple repetition, and younger children seem unaware of this. Moely *et al.* (1969) showed children aged 5 to 11 a collection of pictures of objects which could be grouped into categories. The pictures were laid out in a circle and no two pictures from the same category were put together. The experimenter then told the children to study the pictures, and to rearrange them if they liked, so that they could repeat the names of the objects in the pictures from memory on the experimenter's return. The older children spontaneously rearranged the pictures into groups as an aid to memory, whereas the younger did not do so. This, however, may reflect a lack of knowledge of both mnemonic strategies and classification.

Appel *et al.* (1972) studied groups of children aged 4, 7 and 11. Each child studied a display of cards and was told in one condition to 'look' at the cards and in the other to 'remember' them. The 4-year-olds behaved in the same way in both tasks and remembered the same amount in each; the 7-year-olds did not recall more in the 'memory' condition although they did attempt to adapt their behaviour to the memory requirement; their problem was that although they knew that some effort should be made to aid memory they did not know what. The II-year-olds behaved differently in the memory condition, used appropriate strategies, and remembered more.

Although these laboratory-based experiments may not seem typical of the kind of problem the children would be faced with in the real world, they are similar to some of the demands made on them in school. Soviet researchers, however, have studied memory in more practical contexts. Istomina (1948/1974) tested children aged 3 to 7. All the children had to remember the same five words: in the memory condition they were told simply to remember the words whereas in the play condition the words were presented as a list of items which they had to remember to buy from the shop. Overall the older children remembered more than the younger ones, but all the children remembered more in the play condition. Similarly Wellman (1977) showed that young children will use strategies to help them to remember something, showing that they have some understanding that memory is a process that can be aided. He found them to have an understanding of strategies, such as asking an adult to remind them or writing a note, and also that when younger children tried to remember which cup concealed an object they would touch it and look at it as a way of committing it to memory (Wellman *et al.*, 1975).

As children grow older their ability to use strategies intentionally to aid memorizing develops. Collins and Hagan (1979) argued that at about the age of 5 or 6, once the perceptual processing of information has become automatic, the conscious use of memory processes appears, implying a shift from the perceptual to the conceptual. School-age children are also increasingly able to make use of their knowledge of the world, as well as being able to think about memory itself as being a process which is, to an extent, under their own control (see p. 99).

The development of language

For Piaget language was unlike other aspects of the semiotic function. Other aspects could be totally formed by the child itself as a means of representing the external world, but language is socially transmitted. Thus the mental image is directly related to the external objects signified and is hence, according to Piaget, a 'true symbol', whereas in language the word is merely a socially mediated conventional label attached to the object, or the relationship between objects, and called by Piaget a 'sign'. Within the semiotic function Piaget (1946/1951, 1970a) distinguished three types of 'signifiers' (things that stand for external objects and events): indexes, symbols and signs:

> (a) Indexes are signifiers that are not differentiated from their significants since they are part of them or a causal result, for example, for an infant, hearing a voice is an index of someone's presence. (b) Symbols are signifiers that are differentiated from their significants, but they retain a measure of similarity with them, for example, in a symbols game representing bread by a white stone or vegetables by grass. (c) Signs are signifiers that are also differentiated from their significants, but are conventional and thus more or less 'arbitrary': the sign is always social, whereas the symbol can have a purely individual origin as in symbolic games or dreams. (Piaget, 1970a, p. 116)

It is, however, the individual who gives meaning to the signifiers – they do not, of themselves, represent objects. Therefore they are only valuable in so far as both the speaker's and listener's knowledge allows them to be decoded. This socially transmitted system of signs was thought by Piaget to help children to separate thought and action by enabling them to distinguish between the signifiers, i.e. the words, and that which they signify, i.e. actions, events and objects. Pre-operational children may not appreciate this distinction between symbol and sign, believing that the name of an object is a property of the object which cannot be changed arbitrarily. Children of this age are also thought by Piaget to have difficulty using language to communicate if to do so requires them to take the role of the listener and adapt their own message to take account of what the person they are speaking to does not know. Piaget saw pre-operational children as primarily engaging in 'collective monologues', whereby they speak while alongside one another, but the function of such 'egocentric speech' was not thought to be to communicate but rather to represent children's talking to themselves. Piaget believed that as speech becomes more social such monologues die away, in contrast to Vygotsky (1962) who thought they were internalized and became 'inner

58

speech', the function of which was to regulate behaviour. In older children and adults such inner speech was believed to become externalized again if they became engaged on a particularly awkward or demanding task.

By the end of the pre-school period the child's language development is practically complete, although facility in the use of language, or communicative competence, will continue to develop throughout the life span. When we say that a child has acquired language, as compared with learning a language, we are pointing to the fact that several discrete linguistic skills have been developed and are being co-ordinated to produce an utterance which encodes the speaker's meaning in such a way as to make it possible for the listener to decode it with the minimum of misunderstanding. First, at base, language is composed of separate sounds and intonations of the voice brought about by the use of stress and pauses. This 'phonological' system develops rapidly during infancy (see chapter 1). Secondly, the sounds can be put together to make words which are joined into sentences. This process is regulated by the 'syntactic' system of language, or the rules for relating one sign (or word) to another. Thirdly, the conventional signs of language (words and sentences) convey meaning and the 'semantic' system orders the relationship between the signs and their meanings. Finally, language is essentially a social activity involving dialogue and the mutual apprehension of meaning.

Chomsky (1965) argued that the child has an innate knowledge of syntax, or the rules of structural and grammatical relationships. He believed this must be innate since children produce both syntactically correct sentences which are novel, and hence could not be the result of imitation, and systematic errors in their speech which are not made by adult speakers, and therefore could not have been learned from them. Syntactically, children seem to be speaking a language which is unique to them although comprehensible to adults. Children's first productions usually consist of single words, or two-word utterances, which make them seem like shorthand sentences since all the articles and prepositions have been left out. Braine (1963) believed these to consist of two syntactic categories, 'open' words, which could occur alone, and 'pivot' words, which always occurred with an open word either before or after them. Therefore the child's earliest syntax could produce sentences in three forms: (1) pivot word plus open word, for example 'bye-bye man', 'no bed'; (2) open word plus pivot, for example 'mama come', 'allgone dinner'; and (3) two open words, for example 'find bear', 'milk cup'.

Brown (1973), following Slobin (1971), says children may be using operating principles such as:

Pay attention to the end of words.
Pay attention to the order of words and morphemes.
Underlying semantic relations should be marked overtly and
    clearly. (Brown, 1973, p. 87)

The problem is not that the children do not have complex ideas to express, but that they find the production of such ideas too complex linguistically rather than cognitively. They therefore begin by excluding all unnecessary words so that only that which is new and not redundant is likely to be expressed in words. Later the child will modify a simple noun phrase, such as 'want hat' to 'want Daddy hat', by adding a possessive. These simple sentences are combined, in the second year, and gradually the child becomes able to use adverbs, questions, relatives and conjunctions until, at about the age of 5, the child's syntactic competence is similar to that of an adult's.

Children seem to develop a syntactic system in order to express meaning. The intention to communicate meaning precedes the construction of the appropriate means for so doing. The study of semantic development is the study of how the child comes to understand and produce meaningful utterances. In order to understand the meaning of a sentence the listener must both understand what the individual words mean and also the relationship between them. To know, for example, the person who acts and the person who is acted upon is to understand a semantic relationship between the two, albeit mediated by syntactic order. It seems that children begin with an intention to express a meaning and then find a means of doing so. For example, Cromer (1974), using Bloom's (1970) data, argued that children develop a notion such as negation before being able to express it correctly linguistically.

There seems little point in seeking to communicate meaning unless the child has someone to communicate with. Recently linguists have concentrated on the fact that language, in addition to being socially transmitted, is in essence a social interactive activity, not the autistic egocentric one described by Piaget. Garvey and Hogan (1973) studied eighteen pairs of children aged $3^{1}/_{2}$ to 5 and found many examples of dialogue which required the children to understand what was involved in meaningful linguistic exchanges with another person. Infants lay the foundations for dialogue in their turn-taking communications with their mothers. Once the intention to convey meaning is developed, alongside a simple syntactic means of doing so, the child can build upon this intersubjective communicative experience and develop the ability to hold conversations, with their turn-taking qualities, as well as using language to express needs. Seeing language as a social phenomenon draws attention to the context in which it is acquired. This will affect both the range of experience to which the child is exposed and the nature of his or her production. Parents have been found (by Snow and Ferguson, 1977) to modify their speech to suit their children by speaking slower, more simply and with greater exaggeration of salient aspects than they do with adults. While this is undoubtedly helpful to the children, the greatest influence exerted by adults seems to be when they enable children to express their meaning more clearly, by providing them with a new word, for example, rather than when they attempt to improve their syntax.

The exact relationship between language and thought has been the subject of dispute for decades. So far as we know, only human beings have both language and operational thinking (see p. III) and therefore it seems reasonable to see them as evolving together. The early years of life show rapid development in both capacities, which may point to some reciprocal influence, although the existence of similar developmental schedules does not necessarily imply any such relationship. Piaget (1923/1926, 1963/1969) believed that language and thought were independent. His argument was that if language was a conventional means of representing objects and events, then children must have knowledge of such objects and events *before* they are able to represent them linguistically. At the early stages of life Piaget saw language as neither a necessary nor a sufficient condition for thought; at the concrete and formal stages (see p. 109) it may be necessary but it is still not sufficient. Support for Piaget's view is given by Brown (1973) who saw language as important in enabling an individual to transcend the limits of personal experience by receiving the knowledge gained by others, but he did not believe that human beings' language aided our cognition in an evolutionary sense. Studies of deaf children (Furth and Youniss, 1971) showed that, while their disability does indeed handicap them in tasks which are based on language, in other tasks their performance is comparable with that of hearing children; therefore there appears to be no overall intellectual deficiency but merely a specific deficiency related to language tasks.

An alternative theory (Luria, 1961; Sokolov, 1972; Vygotsky, 1962) is that language is a 'second signalling system' which enables human beings to abstract and generalize information coming from the environment and therefore develop thought and regulate behaviour. For Sokolov, language and thought are one process, with thought beginning when language is internalized and becomes 'inner speech'. However, this implies that language is, initially, external, whereas certainly the semantic aspects of language appear to originate in the subjective inner world of the speaker's intention to communicate his or her meaning. Vygotsky did distinguish between thought and inner speech. For him the latter made the link between thought and the meaning of overt speech. Thus thought grew out of the meaning of words since the child was believed to begin with words which were conceptualized as properties of objects, not merely as conventionally linked to them; Vygotsky held that once the meaning of the word is understood, it is internalized by inner speech and then becomes thought. Thus for Piaget it was actions which were internalized to become the operations of thought, whereas for Vygotsky it was the meaning of words. Luria and Vygotsky believed that the behaviour of young children was dominated by the primary sensory areas of the cortex so that the immediate environment dominated their actions, but by age 4 to 5, however, the secondary signalling system developed so that they could take account of verbal inputs and attend to what they were told rather than to what was perceptually salient. Then children will reach out for the object they are told to get, rather than grasp the object nearest to hand which was a characteristic response of younger subjects.

Bruner (1966b) saw language as an instrument of thought, regarding the child's linguistic organization as setting the parameters for his or her thinking. He believed that 'in order for the child to use language as an instrument of thought, he must first bring the world of experience under the control of principles of organisation that are in some degree isomorphic with the structural principles of syntax' (p. 47). Bruner argued that symbolic activity was species-specific and he saw cognitive development as consisting of ways of representing the world. The first of these, the 'enactive' mode, is characterized by representing the world through action so that it is 'a mode of representing past events through appropriate motor responses' (Bruner, 1973, p. 328). In the 'iconic' mode children aged 2 to 6 replace action with an image or a spatial scheme. Thus images 'stand for' the object, as does a picture or a map. The final, 'symbolic', mode of representation, appearing at about the age of 6 to 7, frees children from the constraints of both their own actions towards objects and the nature of their images. An image is tied to the object it represents whereas the link between a symbol and the thing symbolized is purely conventional. At the symbolic stage the child has moved from representing the world by 'doing' (the enactive period) through 'sensing' (the iconic period) to 'symbolizing' (the symbolic period). At this final stage the child is free from the world of appearances, that is from the present context, and is able to go beyond the information given, which for Bruner is the centre of cognition. This symbolic representation of experience was thought by Bruner to facilitate mature cognition and to be dependent on the verbally based processes of schooling. Simply because it was linguistically based this symbolic representation would determine the forms of thinking it facilitated.

For educationalists the relationship between language and thought has been of considerable interest, particularly as it was believed that 'linguistic deficit' might cause educational failure. This has been difficult to substantiate, largely because 'linguistic deficit' has been difficult to define. Some children are inarticulate, and do not use language to communicate easily, but this does not imply that they cannot do so, nor that their thought is, necessarily, impaired. In any one situation the possibilities are that (1) the child has an inner subjective meaning to express but does not know how to express it, perhaps because of the absence of adequate support from his or her parents in the early stages of dialogue; (2) the child has a meaning to express, knows how to express it, but does not choose to do so when faced with a strange teacher or schoolmates;

(3) the child does not have a clear meaning, or is confused, and a confused linguistic output reflects this; or (4) the child's linguistic problems inhibit the child's thought to such an extent that it reflects the linguistic deficiencies. Exactly which of these is true may vary from situation to situation, but to assume that the child's difficulties always, or ever, stem from the fourth possibility is unwarranted on the evidence available.

The roots of educational competence

Individual differences and environmental influences

We have seen that while children may show less variability in their sensori-motor intelligence than in their later operational intelligence, environmental factors may have a certain influence during the pre-school period. While there is still considerable similarity in children's cognitive behaviour, some differences are beginning to appear which may be significant indicators of later school attainment.

There have been a number of studies which suggest that parents and the general home environment do directly influence their children's cognitive development. However, these studies are difficult to evaluate since, even if a relationship is found between parental behaviours and children's cognition, this does not prove that the relationship is causal. One of the earliest series of such studies were those of Hess and Shipman (1965, 1967) who argued that mothers who helped their children to see the environment as coherent, patterned and meaningful would have children who were more likely to succeed in school. They put forward three arguments which they subsequently tested and found to be generally supportable:

1. The behaviour that leads to societal, educational and economic poverty is socialised in early childhood.
2. The central quality involved in the effects of cultural deprivation is a lack of cognitive meaning in the mother–child communication system.
3. The growth of cognitive processes is fostered in family control systems which offer and permit a wide range of alternatives of action and thought and that such growth is constricted by systems of control which offer pre-

determined solutions and few alternatives for consideration and choice. (Hess and Shipman, 1965, p. 870)

Brophy (1970) found that middle-class mothers would explain a task to their children before they started on it whereas the working-class mother, at least in this sample, only corrected the child when a mistake had been made. However, delayed correction, if the child is thereby made aware of the nature of the mistake by seeing its outcome, was found by Light (1979) to correlate with good role-taking, as was maternal praise and an adequate introduction to the task. He did not find any correlation between maternal teaching style and social class. It may well be that parental style will affect the child's approach to learning, and that certain styles are more characteristic of certain social groups, but class, as such, is unlikely to be determining. Radin (1976) found that fathers' behaviour was correlated with the scores of their 4-year-old sons on an intelligence and vocabulary test, in that boys who had nurturant fathers had higher scores than the sons of fathers who were cool and aloof; however, there was no such effect for girls. Block (1979) offers a possible explanation for this by showing that when children were asked to solve a puzzle while being watched by their fathers, the fathers encouraged the boys to complete the task successfully but subtly discouraged their daughters by stressing social aspects of the situation or playing with and protecting them. If fathers do not stress cognitive competence in their daughters at all, whether or not they are nurturant should not matter.

Hertzig *et al.* (1968) carried out a study of how 3-year-old children behaved when responding to cognitive demands. The children were part of the sample of a longitudinal study of Puerto Rican working-class children living in New York and middle-class American children. The usual contaminating variables seem well controlled in that both groups (116 middle-class and 60 Puerto Rican children) were equally fit at birth and healthy during their first three years and had equally stable families. The working-class group were not materially deprived or part of the 'culture of poverty'. When the children were tested, with the Stanford-Binet revised form known as 'L', half the middle-class and all the working-class children were tested by a psychologist they knew. In the Puerto Rican case the psychologist was Puerto Rican, and

Spanish or English was used in the test depending on the language in which the child was most fluent. The Puerto Rican form of the test was one which had been modified, and translated, for use in Puerto Rico. The researchers were not interested in a child's answers, but in *how* the child approached the test, and to this end an observer watched and recorded the children's behaviour in all testing sessions.

The children's responses were analysed and placed in a series of behaviour categories which did not include any considerations of the underlying reasons for the response. When being asked to carry out a task children could decide to 'work' or 'not work' on the task and this decision could be expressed verbally or non-verbally. Children who decided to work on the task could then either confine themselves to the task or, by spontaneous comments, etc., go beyond the task as set. Children who chose not to work on the task could simply refuse, or engage in other behaviour such as 'rationalisation of competence, substitutive verbalisation or actions, requests for assistance, or passive non-participation' (Hertzig *et al.*, 1968, pp. 11–12). As the testing continued children could modify or maintain their initial stances.

The results showed that the majority of children worked on the tasks rather than refused to do so, but the proportion of work responses was higher in the middle-class group (72 per cent) than in the Puerto Rican group (64 per cent). It was also much more likely in the middle-class group for an initial non-work response to become a work response (53 per cent compared with 42 per cent of Puerto Ricans). The middle-class group was characterized by a verbal mode of expression and the Puerto Rican by a non-verbal mode. Interestingly the middle-class children were as likely to give a work response to a verbal item as to give one to a performance item (82 per cent and 86 per cent respectively) whereas with the Puerto Rican children, while their work-response rate at 85 per cent was similar to that of the middle-class children on the performance items, the difference appeared in the verbal items, where it dropped to 66 per cent. When middle-class children refused to work on a task they accompanied their refusal with some reference to their competence, saying that they could not do the task because, for example, they had not yet learned how to do it. This was a rare response for the Puerto Ricans, who were more likely to give a verbal substitution such as asking for a drink or saying they wished to play with some other toys. A non-verbal refusal from the middle-class children was more likely to take the form of pushing the materials away or shaking their heads and, from the Puerto Ricans, to be shown by passive unresponsiveness.

This pattern of response was maintained when middle-class and Puerto Rican children of matched IQs were compared. However, when the behaviour of children with different IQs within the groups was assessed some interesting results were found. While broadly similar behaviour was found between middle-class children with average (90–110) and higher (116–168) IQs, the average group was significantly less likely to cite lack of competence as a reason for a prior 'not-work' response. They tended to use substitutions, as did the Puerto Rican group. In the Puerto Rican group, children of average IQ, which represented the upper level of their IQ range, were compared with children of lower IQ (90 and below). Here the average group was significantly more likely to work on verbal tasks (75 per cent versus 55 per cent) *and* performance tasks (91 per cent and 75 per cent). While both groups were most likely to express non-verbal non-work responses by passivity, the average-IQ group's responses were otherwise characterized by substitution and the lower IQs by negation. Even though references to competence were rare they were three times more likely in the average group. There were a few significant sex differences for the middle-class group: the girls had a greater proportion of passive non-work responses. The Puerto Rican girls were more likely to give work responses, and express non-work responses passively, while the boys were more likely to follow a work response with a non-work one and express non-verbal refusal to work by a substitute activity.

Throughout this study, while strictly speaking what is being reported is different styles of response to cognitive demands, what comes across is differences between the two groups of children in their responsiveness to this type of situation. Thus, the authors say,

In the middle class group . . . the children would . . . make such remarks as 'I don't know how to do it yet', 'I'm too little to do it', or 'I haven't learned that yet' . . . the most frequent of the verbal non-work responses in the Puerto Rican children was irrelevant substitution which included such statements as 'I want my mummy', 'I want to play with the toys', 'I want to go home' or 'I want a drink of water'. (Hertzig *et al.*, 1968, pp. 40–1)

The middle-class children seemed to understand the situation they were in and be able to reflect on their own ability to think, not just in the present, but in the future, whereas the Puerto Rican children did not seem happy with either the place or the task, or aware of what exactly was going on despite the fact that they both knew, and liked, their testers. The authors suggest that the differences in style may relate to the children's backgrounds. The middle-class background provides a 'problem-oriented culture', in which children are encouraged to develop their own abilities, to complete tasks and to become as independent as their age would allow, whereas the Puerto Ricans have a 'person-oriented culture', which does not stress task-mastery and uses verbal exchanges for affective and social communications rather than task-directed ones. These differences may be affecting these 3-year-olds' understanding of what 'doing a task' means and this will, in turn, affect their performance when they reach school.

While cognitively there may be very little difference between the groups, response styles such as these may well have a disproportionate effect on children's school achievement, in particular on the extent to which they are able to think about their own thinking. The authors conclude that either the Puerto Rican children can be given experiences which will make their attitudes more like those of the middle-class children or 'methods of instruction can be devised that will take into account their characteristic response pattern to demands for cognitive functioning' (p. 51) and favour the latter. This is obviously sensible if, for example, Piaget is right in seeing cognitive development as depending on a process of equilibration. For development will not proceed if equilibrium is not disturbed, and it will not be disturbed if the child does not attempt the task. If teachers are to attempt to adapt instruction to the work style of their pupils, they need to ensure that such adaptations do not render the instruction inefficient by removing from it those very aspects which would foster cognitive growth. The means of instruction may well need to be varied but its cognitive content will have to be retained.

Carey (1974) did not believe that cognitive competence could be related to social class *per se*. In her view cognition was based on a series of sub-skills which the individual could acquire or fail to acquire. Failure would lead to cognitive difficulties but she argued that the cause of that failure was lack of opportunity to acquire the sub-skills not lack of ability to do so. However, the effect of failing to acquire such sub-skills could be cumulative and hence, in her view, pre-school experience should enable the child to develop these basic sub-skills. Bruner (1974) argued that children will develop skills during play when they can perfect their schemes in comparative safety during their long period of immaturity. Observational learning was, he thought, the traditional way such skills were passed on via modelling and practice in play. Today much skilled adult behaviour takes place at work, when the child is not present and hence lacks the opportunity for informal, observational learning. Thus schools become necessary.

Early childhood education

While there is a general belief that early childhood education is valuable, it does not seem to be thought valuable enough to allocate resources to it in preference to other areas of education, nor is it clear what its main purpose is. Is it to aid the child's social development through fostering interaction with strange adults and peers? Or is it to accelerate cognitive development? Is the aim to prepare the child for school or to make good real, or imagined, deficits in the child's experience to date? Perhaps pre-school provision should be made simply to provide a place of safety and stimulation for a child whose parents are working. Or perhaps it should have no aim beyond that of providing an environment in which a child can be a child. This last aim is unlikely to be clearly articulated since few people, other than Rousseau, have fully accepted the implications of the view that childhood could be a state in its own right. Children are usually seen as being prepared for a future state, or as developing towards future maturity, and so childhood is not held to represent the completion of any process. While adults are allowed to 'be', the emphasis in childhood is almost inevitably, if sadly, on 'becoming'.

There have been some attempts to base early childhood education programmes on Piagetian theory (Kamii and De Vries, 1976, 1977; Weikart *et al.*, 1971). Generally, Piaget's views on the role of activity in the construction of knowledge and his stage theory have been more influential than his theory of equilibration, although the latter is the most central. Kamii (1981) maintained that 'as an educator the most fundamental point I get out of the books by Piaget is that of constructivism by equilibration' (p. 235). This led her to list three short-term objectives for early education:

1. In relation to adults
   we would like children to develop their autonomy through relationships in which adult power is reduced to a minimum.
2. In relation to peers
   we would like children to develop their ability to decenter and co-ordinate different points of view.
3. In relation to learning
   we would like children to be alert, curious, confident in their ability to figure things out, and say what they honestly think. We would also like them to have initiative, come up with interesting ideas, problems, and questions, and put things into relationships. (pp. 241–2)

She believed that a programme based on Piagetian notions, i.e. a constructivist programme, would differ fundamentally from other instructional programmes, and she offered a programme for what teachers can actually do in the classroom which related classroom activities to Piagetian forms of knowledge (table 1).

The headings are more or less self-evident, but she does remind the reader of the important point that while physical knowledge means knowledge of the properties of objects, to which the child must accommodate his or her schemes, logico-arithmetical knowledge is 'in the child'. This is true in the sense that to see two objects as 'the same' or 'different' is to draw attention to something which *exists* in neither of the objects but which follows from the cognitive act of considering them together. For example, take

the simplest relationship between two objects such as a red bead and a green one of the same size, both made of wood. The two beads can be considered 'different'. In this situation, the relationship 'different' exists neither in the red bead nor in the green one, nor anywhere else in external reality. (Kamii, 1981, p. 247)

Table 1   Child-development curriculum activities reconceptualized with Piaget's theory

Child-development curriculum activities	Physical knowledge	Social knowledge	Logico-arithmetical knowledge			Knowledge of space and time		Representation		
			Classification	Seriation	Number	Spatial reasoning	Temporal reasoning	Index	Symbol	Sign
Dramatic play		X					X		X	X
Block building	X					X			X	
Painting	X					X			X	
Other arts and crafts activities	X					X			X	
Caring for animals and plants	X						X			
Cooking	X						X			
Singing and playing musical instruments	X	X				X				X
Movement						X			X	
Listening to stories		X				X	X		X	X
Sand and water play	X									
Playing with playground equipment	X					X				
Table games (e.g. puzzles)						X			X	
Group games (e.g. Musical Chairs)		X								

Source: Kamii, 1981, p. 235.

Programmes based on a theory such as Piaget's, which stresses that cognitive change is based on the process of equilibration and delimits certain characteristics of child thought, would need to bear in mind the fact that the more cognitively immature the children, the more inconsistent their thinking will be and the more they will 'cast around' for help in finding a solution. Children's greater sensitivity to context is a measure of their immaturity. However, this should be seen as a positive behaviour since by this means children will become aware of the differences between relevant and irrelevant dimensions to problems. Given this possible contextual sensitivity in pre-school children, the teacher needs to ensure that the context does not include misleading contextual cues and at the same time to provide opportunities for children to experience cognitive conflict and thereby restructure their schemes. Conflict is positive when it is planned, intended and appropriate for the developmental stage of the child concerned. If there is no conflict there will be no need to restructure and hence no development, but if the context of the task set for the child contains too much confusing information the child will merely remain confused.

With respect to the role of activity, it is essential to remember that mere activity is insufficient; only activity plus reflection will lead to a reconstruction of cognitive structures. This is because activity plus reflection may lead to disequilibrium and thereby initiate the process of equilibration.

It has been argued that early childhood education generally does little to accelerate a child's cognitive development or to compensate for cognitive deficits and that any cognitive benefits that are detectable are likely to be temporary (Belsky and Steinberg, 1978; Bronfenbrenner, 1974; Chazan, 1978). Certain forms of intervention, however, have been found to have an effect. Tizard (1978) pointed out that

> children in *good* residential nurseries talk and understand speech like ordinary children of ordinary working-class parents; but children in *very* good ones, linguistically speaking, talk and understand speech like children of professional parents. Again, children who are brought up at home by mothers with IQs less than 70 have IQs of about 95 between the ages of two and six; but similar children who attend a stimulating all-day nursery centre from early infancy have IQs of 120. These and other data show that environmental differences if great enough, *can* result in profound differences in competencies. (pp. 153–4)

As the child approaches the age of 5 and the start of compulsory schooling the intuitive world of pre-operational thought is about to be replaced by operational thinking, and formal instruction will soon begin. If children's experiences during the first five years have enabled them to realize that their environment is ordered, potentially comprehensible and able to be affected in predictable ways by their actions, they will be ready for the major demands the next stage will make on their maturing cognitive processes.

4

The first school (5–8)

In Britain the age of 5 marks the start of compulsory schooling.
Obviously before this age the average child has been learning,
both intentionally and unintentionally, but it is only once the child
has reached 5 that the state insists that he or she shall leave home
for several hours each day, be placed with a qualified 'teacher' in a
specialized institution together with other children of the same
chronological but not necessarily mental age and follow a particular curriculum. The aim of this schooling is usually said to be to
facilitate the child's cognitive, social and emotional development,
with the greatest emphasis, implicitly if not explicitly, on the first
of these aspects. To achieve these aims a curriculum is devised
which is based on what is considered desirable for children to
know and taking into account their age, ability and aptitudes. If the
curriculum devised is to meet the children's needs it must
consider not only how they will think, but also how they are
thinking and how this thinking is influenced by their current social
and emotional development. In order to facilitate development the
content and methods of instruction must start from where chil-

dren actually are and, building upon this, enable them to move forward.

Such considerations are particularly crucial when planning for children in infant departments since they are at the point of transition from 'pre-school' to 'school' children. Although patterns of behaviour which may predispose the child to success or failure in this new environment may already have been laid down (Turner, 1980), the majority of children of this age are in fact all equally illiterate and innumerate. Therefore the more appropriate the curriculum, the more likely it will be that the children will develop basic skills, and those who come expecting failure may, by early success, come to reassess their outlook.

Perspectives on the transition to operational thinking

During these years children move from their more simple response to the world, primarily in terms of actions and images, to a response which requires an ability to symbolize generally, to use internal cognitive mediators and, ultimately, to reflect upon the relations between symbols. White (1965) found changes between the ages 5 and 7 in twenty-one different behaviours. There are various theories as to what is involved in this shift of thinking. Although the dividing line between childhood and adulthood has been drawn at different ages in different cultures and historical periods (Ariés, 1962; Tucker, 1977), there is a large measure of agreement that in certain ways children are different from adults and that the age of 7 marks a turning point, as does puberty. At puberty adult sexuality emerges; the age of 7 is often seen as the moment when the child begins to 'reason'. Rousseau, whose philosophical treatise on childhood, *Émile* (1762/1911), indicates that he observed at least young children with considerable care, commented that

childhood is the sleep of reason . . . before the age of reason the child receives images, not ideas; and this is the difference between them: images are merely the pictures of external objects, while ideas are notions about those objects determined by their relations. . . . I maintain, therefore, that as children are incapable of judging, they have no true memory. They retain sounds, form, sensation, but rarely ideas and still more rarely

75

relations. You tell me they acquire some rudiments of geometry, and you think you prove your case; not so, it is mine you prove; you show that far from being able to reason themselves, children are unable to retain the reasoning of others; for if you follow the method of these little geometricians you will see they only retain the exact impression of the figure and the terms of the demonstration. They cannot meet the slightest new objection; if the figure is reversed they can do nothing. All their knowledge is on the sensation level, nothing has penetrated to their understanding. (pp. 71–2)

Piaget's ideas (1924/1926, 1964/1980) seem strikingly similar to Rousseau's. Piaget too believed that the development of 'concrete operations' marked a qualitative shift in the thinking of children of this age in that they moved from the intuitive world of pre-operational intelligence to the period of concrete operations in which their thinking became governed by 'operations' or internalized actions which are reversible and governed by laws (see p. 105). For Piaget this transition occurred because the child constructed new cognitive structures through the process of equilibration. Piaget's view is best understood by considering his account of the development of specific concepts (see p. 80).

In contrast to Piaget, other researchers do not see the shift in thinking between 5 and 7 as being the result of structural change, rather they see it as reflecting more discrete behavioural changes. For example the Kendlers (see p. 4) saw the shift as being from a form of thinking that could be modelled by single unit theory to one which could best be described by mediation theory.

Similar to this was Stevenson's (1970) and White's (1970) work on transpositional problems, in which children aged 3 to 7 were shown two circles A and B; B was 1 inch larger in diameter than A and the children were taught always to choose the larger of the two, i.e. B. Then A was removed and a new circle C was presented to the children which was one inch bigger than B. The younger children continued to choose B whereas the older ones, realizing that the task was to choose the larger in the pair, chose C. That is, in these tasks, the older children responded to the relative sizes of the circles. However, these findings were reversed by Bryant (1972, quoted in Bryant 1974). He showed 4-year-olds pairs of cards arranged so that in the first pair one card had ten figures on it and the other card twelve, and in the second pair one card had twelve figures and the other fourteen, and trained the children either to pick the card with most figures on it in each pair, or the card with twelve figures on it. The younger children found the relative task, i.e. picking the card with the most figures, easier. This suggests that they were able to use the mediating response 'larger than' but did not have the abstract concept 'twelve' and hence could not use it as a mediator. To this extent Piaget's work, which stresses the importance of structures, is, arguably, more explanatory of cognitive change than that of others who do not accept the existence of internal structures, in that, while the use of mediators may be important, their availability may itself depend on the child's level of cognitive development. Hence abstract mediators may not be able to be used before the child has developed the relevant 'formal' or 'abstract' structure which is a precondition for using such mediators.

A third view is that as the child becomes better able to discriminate aspects of the problem relevant for its solution so his or her performance will improve. Tighe and Tighe (1972) argued that once children confronted with a reversal-shift problem become aware that 'colour' is a relevant dimension they can perform a reversal shift, but while they see each part of the task as a separate problem they will not see any relationship between their previous response and their subsequent one. The Tighes therefore trained 4- and 5-year-olds to become aware of the dimensions relevant for a reversal shift by making them attend to the extent that one stimulus was the same or different from a previous one. These trained children, it was shown, found reversal shifts easier than did a matched group of untrained children. Attention has also been found to be significant for the development of the concept of conservation (see p. 83).

Both McGarrigle and Donaldson (1974) and Light *et al.* (1979) drew attention to the difficulties the child may have in the testing situation itself and saw the 5–7 shift as reflecting the child's greater cognitive autonomy. McGarrigle and Donaldson believed that in the traditional conservation task (see p. 89) the child paid more attention to the non-verbal behaviour of the experimenter than to what was said, since in the early stages of language acquisition the child may pay more attention to the context of an utterance than to the words themselves, only arriving at an understanding of the speaker's meaning through interpreting the speaker's behaviour. Later, in the pre-school and early school years, the child may be able to attend to language *per se* provided there is no conflict between what is said and what is done, but where such a conflict exists the child will revert to paying attention to the speaker's behaviour. They concluded:

> It is possible that the achievements of the concrete operational stage are as much a reflection of the child's increasing independence from features of the interactional setting as they are evidence of the development of a logical competence. (McGarrigle and Donaldson, 1974, p. 349)

Here McGarrigle and Donaldson liken the child's developing comprehension of language to adults learning a foreign language. This could not account for the child's *production* of language which, as we have seen, reflects the child's semantic intentions. However, comprehension may rely more heavily on context which would indicate that the child can, with appropriate contextual support, comprehend more than he or she can produce.

Light *et al.* (1979), having replicated McGarrigle and Donaldson and carried out a study of their own (see p. 90), also concluded that the child had to learn to divorce the meaning of words from the meaning of the context in which they were used. Such a divorce requires the child to pay selective attention to the linguistic aspects of the task and supports the view that children need to learn to discriminate the relevant aspects of a problem and attend to them alone.

The approaches discussed so far suggest that cognitive development is a smooth progression from a less to a more adequate mode of response, but this may not be so. Very young children may appear to 'conserve' but this is simply because they have not noticed the perceptual change. Non-conservation is their first attempt to make sense of the perceptual change (see p. 91). Similarly Karmiloff-Smith (1979) found that 3-year-old French children use the French word *un* correctly, whether they use it in the sense of 'a' or 'one', because they had not realized the distinction. When, at about 5, they do realize that it has two meanings they use it, correctly, as 'a' but use *une de* for 'one'. Finally, they once again use the word correctly in both contexts but are, this time, aware of the double usage.

Thornton (1982) found a similar effect in classification in that 5-year-olds and 10-year-olds appeared to sort objects similarly and as effectively, whereas 7-year-olds did not. Her explanation is that similarity of outcome in the sorting procedures of the 5- and 10-year-olds should not be taken as indicating a similarity of procedure. Five-year-olds are quite capable of putting red circles and squares together to form the class of 'red' objects, and blue circles and squares to form the class of 'blue' objects, but these two correct sortings are simply, in Thornton's terminology, 'juxta-posed' since the child does not realize that there is an alternative classificatory scheme of 'squares' and 'circles' and that these four potential classes are interrelated. She tested children between the ages of 5 and 10 on a constrained card-sorting task. The children had to sort twelve cards, which varied with respect to colour, shape and pattern, into four boxes, each of which would only hold three cards, and were instructed that the cards in each box had to be 'the same in some way'. Success involved filling all the boxes with no more than three cards and having no cards left over, and could only be achieved by using the correct variable (e.g. colour). She found that the children used three procedures to correct unsuccessful first attempts at sorting. In type A the child would leave the groups of cards which had filled a box, or boxes, untouched and only attempt to regroup the cards that were left over. In type B the child would still leave one class uncorrected but would use the other cards to form other groups, employing different criteria and thus showing some awareness that classifications can be changed in response to constraints and hence of the interdependence of classes. The children's behaviour was not systematic in type B. In type C the children, realizing that their original sorting procedure was incorrect, because the outcome was incorrect, would rearrange all the cards thus exhibiting their under-standing of the classes' mutual interdependence. While children of different ages were found to use all three procedures, each was more characteristic of one age group than of the others (i.e. type A was characteristic of the 5-year-olds, type B of the 7-year-olds, and type C of the 10-year-olds). Karmiloff-Smith's and Thornton's work draws attention to the important fact that similar outcomes may reflect the use of different modes of cognitive processing. Only the latter can truly reveal cognitive development.

79

The development of specific forms of understanding

Classification

Inhelder and Piaget (1959/1964) studied children's understanding of classification and divided it into developmental stages according to the types of classification the children made and the processes they used. The youngest children were found to have no ideas of a class and merely to make a 'collection' of objects. These developed into 'chains' of objects in which the child might put a red circle with a red square but follow this with a green square. 'Thematic groupings' would follow when objects were put together on the basis of some functional relationship such as a knife with a fork or a chair with a table. The pre-operational child did not appreciate that one object can be a member of more than one class, for example that a red square can be both a member of the class of red objects and of square objects, or that subordinate classes, for example roses and daffodils, combined together, will form the superordinate class of flowers which can, in turn, be combined with trees to form another superordinate class of plants. However, by the start of the concrete stage the children were found to have developed systems of classification and relationship. First, they understood the combinatorial systems of addition of classes whereby subordinate classes such as primroses and bluebells can be combined to form the superordinate category of flowers. Secondly, they could carry out cross-classifications so that, for example, four blue circles, four blue squares, four red circles, four red squares, can be classified both by number and shape, a feat which children below 7 find difficult. Thirdly, they would realize that classes can intersect so that certain elements can be members of both classes.

Voelin's work (quoted by Vuyk, 1981) led to the conclusion that children aged 5 to 10 years can give a correct answer to class-inclusion problems on an empirical basis when the test material was in front of them, but they lacked a feeling of logical necessity and failed in abstract problems. They succeeded in the traditional class-inclusion question which requires the child to say when looking at, for example, a bunch of roses and a bunch of daffodils, whether altogether there are more roses or more flowers when the flowers were physically present, but failed when asked whether there were more daisies or more flowers in the forest when, obviously, 'the forest' was not present and had to be thought about by the child. Before the age of 11, children who succeeded with the class-inclusion question would fail with the question 'How can I make it so that there are as many marguerites as flowers?' Younger children appeared to understand collections, for example 'forest /family/army', before classes and they could understand logical necessity with collections before classes. In general, recent research shows that the logico-mathematical structures supposed to be constructed by 7 or 8 years of age still require empirical support. The child only becomes truly concrete-operational at about 10 years of age, at least with respect to classification and seriation.

Seriation

In addition to classifying objects as members of a class, objects within a class have to be related to each other if they possess qualities in varying degrees; the nature of this relationship depends on the degree of their possession of the quality. For example, a group of people may vary in height and thus, if height is the property in question, they can be arranged in order from the smallest to the tallest. This serial ordering, or 'seriation', is beyond the understanding of the young child since it requires the recognition that John can be *both* taller than Peter and shorter than Mark.

In order to seriate, the child has to learn to make a series of the individual objects in a set in such a way that the series will reflect the dimensions along which the objects vary. Piaget's best-known experiment (Piaget and Szeminska, 1941/1952) required children to order a series of sticks of graduated length. He found three developmental stages. At the first, children fail to make the series; at the second, aged 5 to 6, they use trial-and-error methods and may succeed but have particular difficulty understanding that B can be both smaller than A and larger than C. Also, not having developed a system of relationships, they are not able to insert an additional stick into the series once it is completed. Finally, they can create the series with each stick correctly placed and understood to be both bigger than the shorter sticks on one side and smaller than the longer sticks on the other.

Number

Piaget's early work on the concept of number (Piaget and Sze-minska, 1941/1952) is divided into three parts: the first concerns conservation, the second one-to-one correspondence and the third classification. Thus, for Piaget, an understanding of number involves the child in developing simultaneously the notions of conservation, or the understanding that defining properties of an object will remain invariant despite perceptual changes, seriation and classification and the ability to unite these operations to express relations – all part of what Piaget called 'logico-mathematical operations'. In order to develop the concept of number the child must be able to understand that any number, e.g. 7, is a conventional sign representing a class of seven units which need to be ordered as first, second, third, etc., in order to confirm that there are, indeed, seven. This 'ordination' requires the ability to seriate. However, the cardinal number 7 refers to a class, which contains the serially ordered seven units, and it, in turn, relates to the other subordinate classes of six units, nine units, etc., which can be combined into superordinate classes by addition just as they can be broken down into their discrete units, each of which could compose a sub-class of its own. These forms of understanding both singly and in combination seem, except in the simplest of circumstances, to elude young children. In particular, they cannot see the 'formal' nature of the problems or the necessity of the fact that if, for example, $2 + 2 = 4$, then $4 - 2$ must equal 2. They may well get single questions correct, especially if they concern familiar objects or items, but an understanding that *all* questions in this form will be solved in this way, irrespective of content, is lacking. Indeed it may be that their future 'formal' understanding is the result of many particular understandings out of which they may, finally, deduce a general rule. Piaget argued that the concept of number will accompany the development of a general understanding of conservation, for him the basis of all rationality, together with the particular understanding of classification and seriation. Such understandings would involve the reorganization of cognitive structures and it was this that constituted cognitive development.

Conservation

This concept has proved particularly popular with researchers. Brainerd (1978) remarked that the editors of *Child Development* receive more papers on conservation than on any other topic. Gruber and Vonéche (1977) asked: 'is [this] because there is some special mystery in the universal discovery by children of an idea that is neither taught in school nor visible to the senses?' (p. 345). There is no doubt that it holds a particular position in a child's cognitive development since, as Pinard (1981), following Piaget, argued, conservation is a 'polymorphic concept':

> it can be seen that the conservation concept extends far beyond the few privileged domains to which it is customarily restricted. Without loss to its essential meaning, which is the invariance of physical and logical properties of objects in the face of apparent changes brought about by the actions the subject performs on these objects, or by the interactions arising between the various objects, conservation is the very heart of all concepts the child constructs. (pp. 4–5)

And again:

> Conservation is not really a notion to be acquired in the same sense as other notions or concepts such as space, number, time, quantity, etc. It is neither a principle nor a specific cognitive operation but is situated at the centre of each of the logical and spatio temporal concepts the child has to acquire. (p. 148)

It is this that is at the bottom of children's difficulties with conservation. Conservation means the understanding that certain attributes, such as number, substance, weight, volume and identity of objects or people will remain invariant, i.e. be conserved, despite apparent, often perceptual, changes which have no bearing on the attribute in question.

Piaget's theory   Piaget saw conservation as the centre of rationality and carried out a series of experiments on this concept over a number of years. The form of the experiments was described by Piaget and Inhelder (1963a/1969):

> The subject is shown a ball of clay and asked to make another ball of the same size and weight. One ball, *A*, is left on the table

as evidence and the other is transformed into a sausage, a pancake, a number of pieces etc. The subject is asked first whether there is still the same amount of substance in B as in A and why. The procedure is the same whether the child answers 'yes' or 'no'. In either case his answer and the reason that he gives ... serve to prompt further modifications of the object. ... This is done to see whether he will continue to reason in the same way or will change his opinion. The stage that the child has reached is noted (no conservation of substance, ungeneralised and uncertain conservation, or necessary conservation) and also the kind of arguments he uses. One then passes to the conservation of weight. ... Questions are asked about the same transformation as in the case of substance ... but the child is asked whether or not the weight remains the same. ... Finally, the same questions are asked about the conservation of volume. (p. 157)

Piaget claimed to have obtained three kinds of result from these experiments:

In the first place, three successive stages can be observed in the case of each of the notions studied. At first there is a lack of conservation when the object is modified. This is followed by transitional reactions (conservation is assumed but without certainty and in the case of some conservations only). Finally it comes to be affirmed and regarded as evident throughout the various transformations of the ball of clay. Secondly we find that three arguments are advanced by the child on reaching the third stage and these are characteristic of an operational approach ... these three arguments do not correspond to three sub-stages but are interdependent and do not always appear in the same order. The first is based on simple reversibility: there is in B as much (substance, weight or volume) as in A because the ball A can be remade from B. The second rests on a more subtle kind of reversibility (or reversibility through 'reciprocity' as distinct from simple reversibility or reversibility through 'inversion') based on compensation: object B is longer but thinner etc. ... The third argument appears less sophisticated and is simply based on identity: the quantity (or the weight etc.) does not change 'because it's the same stuff', 'because it has only been rolled', ... 'because nothing has been taken away or added.' The remarkable character of this identity is that it ranks as an argument of conservation only when the other two arguments have been discovered. . . . In the third place the results obtained . . . show a time lag between the child's acquisition of the notion of the conservation of substance (toward the age of 8), or weight (age 9–10), and of volume (age 11–12). (pp. 158–9).

The above Piagetian experiment can be seen to consist of five or six steps, shown here with reference to the conservation of continuous quantity:

Step 1: two objects A and B are presented to the child. They are identical with respect to amount of material (attribute x), shape (attribute y) and disposition, being the same height, width, etc. (attribute z).

Step 2: the child compares the objects and they are altered until the child agrees that they are identical with respect to attribute x. No mention is made of attributes y and z. Thus:

$$A_{xyz} = B_{xyz}$$

Step 3: attributes y and z are changed in object B by the action of the experimenter in the sight of the child so that

$$B_{xyz} \rightarrow B^1_{xy^1z^1}$$

Step 4: the child is asked whether

$$A_{xyz} = B^1_{xy^1z^1}$$

Step 5: the child is asked to justify the response.
Step 6: counter-suggestions may be made.

The results of all the experiments are said to show that:

1 The notion of conservation develops in three stages.
2 The conserving child gives three forms of justification in step 5: reversibility, compensation and identity.
3 There is a time lag, or horizontal décalage, between the development of different types of conservation.

These experiments, the results obtained and Piaget's interpretation of the results have led to a considerable amount of further research by Piaget, his supporters and others. In a later work (1974/1980) Piaget studied children's understanding of contradictions and this enabled him to develop further his interpretation of the way in which children construct their conservation schemes. A series of experiments led to the conclusion that the young child attends to the positive aspects of a problem or stimulus and disregards the negative. Once Piaget had centred on the notion of the asymmetry in the child's understanding of affirmation and negation he was able to consider their development as separate at first but finally merging as a mutually compensatory scheme. He then reconsidered the nature of the problem faced by the non-conserver and the path from non-conservation to conservation.

> it is necessary to remember that if one adds material to the length dimension, one is taking it away from somewhere else, and that, in consequence, the sausage is not simply 'longer' by quantity x but also 'less something else', that is, less −x in relation to the previous shape ... the cause of the disequilibrium specific to non-conservations is not only to be sought in the difficulty of keeping two modifications in mind at once while looking at the result of an action or actions: it derives at a much deeper level from the limitations involved in acquiring consciousness of the central action itself, of which the positive aspect linked to its aim (increasing the length, and so on) is alone retained, while the subtractive or negative aspect inseparable from it is disregarded, since only one action, and only one set of elements modified by it, are involved. (Piaget, 1974/1980, p. 189)

Critique on Piaget's theory   The Piagetian conservation tasks have been criticized by a number of researchers. They argue that the Piagetian task does not just test the child's understanding of conservation but, on the contrary, makes other demands upon the child's cognitive skills, and that failure in these latter areas may be, wrongly, interpreted as failure to conserve. Several of these critics then recast the Piagetian task to exclude what are seen as additional hurdles and therefore claim to be testing the child's understanding of conservation uncontaminated by extraneous variables.

In the first of these types of study it is argued that children's difficulties with the aspects of the task may 'cloak' their competence in conservation. Two such difficulties are the task's linguistic bias, in general, and the vocabulary used, in particular.

Donaldson and Wales (1970) showed that children had difficulties with words such as 'less', 'more' and 'same' and concluded that

> children's failure to respond appropriately in tasks in which they are instructed to perform in accord with such talk as 'different from', 'more than', 'is there more here or more here?' and the like may be as attributable to the structure of the child's language as to other aspects of his cognitive apparatus. (p. 265)

Obviously if a child, literally, does not understand what the words 'more', 'less' and 'same' or 'amount' mean, then he or she will not be able to carry out the task. However, it has been argued that, leaving vocabulary aside, the whole linguistic bias of the task creates difficulties for children. In an attempt to obviate the linguistic problem there have been a number of attempts to assess conservation non-verbally. For example, Wheldall and Poborca (1980) tested children's understanding of the conservation of liquid quantity. They carried out three experiments which essentially involved training children, with a mean age of 6½ years, to press a button when they were shown two jars which contained equal amounts of water and not to press the button when the amounts were unequal. When the children were able to do this the water from one of the jars previously judged to be equal was poured into a differently shaped jar, and the children had again to press or refrain from pressing the button. They were also given a traditional verbal test of conservation. None of those who conserved on the verbal paradigm failed on the non-verbal task and significantly more appeared to conserve in the non-verbal than in the verbal condition. There are, however, problems with this type of study. In a press/non-press condition the child has a 50 per cent chance of being correct on any one trial if he or she presses at random. If the children are not asked for reasons for the judgement it is impossible to know, with certainty, *why* they responded as they did and hence equally impossible to judge whether or not they were exhibiting operational behaviour. However, neither does verbal failure necessarily imply non-operational behaviour. Non-verbal studies similar to this are promising and the design would not be affected if children were to be asked why they had responded as they did.

Murray (1981) too took up the problem of how the child initially determines that the objects or arrays are equal and the relationship between this and the child's ability to conserve. He found that a child's knowledge of the 'procedures for making things the same and different' did indeed distinguish conservers from non-conservers and concluded that 'the data provided evidence for the hypothesis that the child's knowledge of the effects of the various testing actions on the properties of objects is a necessary condition, but probably not a sufficient condition, for the conservation of the properties' (p. 159). There is a real difficulty here in that the procedures used by the child for assessing the initial equality, and tacitly accepted by the experimenter, may well cue the child into a false system for judging equality which is subsequently applied after the transformation. Yet if the experimenter queries the child's criteria at this stage by saying, for example, 'But would that *really* alter the amount?', then this too may influence the child and constitute training.

Other studies argue that the child may be positively distracted, or misled, by aspects of the conservation task which are unrelated to conservation competence. These distracters are seen to stem from the fact that the task is a social setting and therefore both the behaviour of the experimenter and, more importantly, the child's interpretation of this behaviour must be taken into account. The traditional task assumes that the task the experimenter is setting is the same task that the child is doing. These studies cast doubt on that initial assumption.

We have seen that children may have vocabulary difficulties and may produce less than optimal performance because of the linguistic bias of the tasks. However, the language problem may be even more extensive in that the child may be linguistically cued into the wrong response. First, the form of the question asked by the experimenter may distract the child in that its very wording may suggest one answer rather than another. Children have been found to appear to conserve more frequently if the questions contained the word 'same' rather than 'more', and to be more likely to conserve if they are asked if the two task components are 'the same' rather than 'if one has more'. However, this may well be because of the recency effect, whereby the child repeats or agrees with the last thing the experimenter said or, when in doubt, acquiesces and says 'Yes'. Secondly, the number and sequence of the questions may be confusing, especially the fact that the child is asked a question after the experimenter has transformed the material and may therefore be led to believe that he or she is expected to say that they are no longer the same. Rose and Blank (1974) devised a one-judgement task, arguing that

the child is asked to make two judgements – one before and one after the rearrangement of the objects before him. In the normal (non-experimental) course of events, however, one would never ask the identical question twice if a significant change had not occurred in the material that was being observed. (p. 499)

The children, with a mean age of 6 years 3 months, were initially divided into three groups. The first group did a standard conservation task; the second saw the array transformed but was only asked whether the rows contained the same number of objects after the transformation; and the third was only shown a fixed array and asked whether the rows were the same to control for the effect of asking just one question. Groups 1 and 3 had equal difficulty whereas group 2 made significantly fewer errors, thus showing that one question asked in a meaningful context did facilitate performance. In a further study it was shown that children who received the one-judgement task first subsequently made less errors on the standard task than those who had been given the standard task alone; indeed this latter group then made more errors on the one-judgement task than the former. Rose and Blank conclude that

the implicit contextual cues which the child first encounters play a large role in determining the response he will employ on this and all subsequent related tasks . . . the results suggest that the role of context . . . is . . . important, since the identical question led to very different results when it was placed in different contexts. (p. 502)

These findings are in line with those of McGarrigle and Donaldson (1974), who argued strongly that the children's behaviour was influenced by their interpretation of the experimenter's behaviour. They began their study from a particular view of language-acquisition, namely that children learn language initially by taking account of the mother's intentions, as expressed non-verbally, and mapping these understandings on to their linguistic means of expression. Therefore in the conservation-of-number task the experimenter's action of moving the counter may lead the child to infer an intention on the experimenter's part that the child should talk about the experimenter's previous action rather than answer his verbal questions, since the experimenter's non-verbal behaviour may be more salient for the child than his verbal request. They therefore devised a task in which the rearrangement of the counters appeared to be accidental, in that a 'naughty teddy bear' disturbed them, and therefore would not be interpreted by the child as a deliberate action by the experimenter. The results showed that more children 'conserved' in the accidental than in the standard condition. Justifications were not required. Their conclusion was that 'It is possible that the achievements of the concrete operational stage are as much a reflection of the child's increasing independence from features of the interactional setting as they are evidence of the development of a logical competence' (p. 350).

Light *et al.* (1979) also found a weaker effect in their replication and they argued that in the accidental condition the children were picking up another non-verbal message, namely that they should ignore the rearrangement. Therefore if the standard condition gives rise to false negatives, i.e. saying that children cannot conserve when they can, the accidental condition gives rise to false positives, i.e. saying that children can conserve when they cannot. Accordingly they used a new incidental condition in which the children in pairs prepared to play a game in which equivalence of amount of pasta shells in each child's beaker was important. The experimenter then 'noticed' a chip in one beaker and poured the shells from that to another, differently shaped beaker. The children were asked whether the amount was the same. Of the children who were the first to be questioned in their pair, 14 'conserved' and 6 did not, compared with 1:19 in the standard condition. Light *et al.* conclude that operativity requires the child to separate the meaning of words from the meaning of the context in which they are spoken. It is clear that in those situations in which the transformation appears more natural and less salient, the child appears to conserve. The problem remains, however, that if the child has not attended to the transformation at all then his or her apparently 'conserving' response means that the child has not realized that there is a 'situation' to deal with, rather than that he or she has dealt with it. This is a difficulty inherent in all studies which attempt to remove cues that may distract the child in that the task itself may be lost, together with the distracting cues.

Perhaps the most pertinent finding in this context was Karmiloff-Smith's (quoted in Vuyk, 1981, p. 391). She showed by analysing the eye movements of children under 3 in a test of conservation of number that they do not look at the end of the array and hence do not see the extension after the transformation. When they do notice this, at about the age of 4, they become non-conservers. Clearly, if no problem is seen to exist the child will have no difficulty in 'conserving'. Non-conservation represents an attempt to solve a problem which has been perceived by the child. Conservation may mean either that a correct solution has been arrived at or that no problem has been recognized as requiring a solution. Hence the need for justifications or explanations of apparently conserving responses.

The mode of presentation may also be distracting. In Fluck and Hewison's (1979) study forty-six 5-year-olds were divided into three groups. The first group received a standard number-conservation task. The second saw the same procedure carried out on a video film by a woman of similar age to the experimenter, but the question was asked by the experimenter who was watching the film with the children. The third group saw a video film of three puppets, in which one 'presented each of the others with a row of six inch cubes in one to one correspondence. The two recipients then proceeded to play with their "bricks" . . . they then began to quarrel over who had more' (p. 508). A dispute between all three puppets ensued in which the donor puppet said they both had the same but the other two denied this. The experimenter then asked the children which puppet had more or if they had the same, and asked for reasons for their answers. The results showed that significantly more children conserved in the puppet condition than in either of the two others, and that there was a relationship between mode of presentation and number of conservers: 21 per cent conserved in the control condition, 53 per cent in the television/adult condition and 71 per cent in the television/puppet condition. They argued that in the puppet condition the child was 'an outsider witnessing a dispute between three characters quite different from himself and the experimenter, but similar to each other. This detached role seems to have enabled most children to apprehend the formal nature of the problem without hindrance from apparently conflicting interpersonal cues' (p. 508).

This is an interesting study which takes into account both the mode of presentation and the social context of the experiment. In addition, the conservation problem is clearly posed. There is however one difficulty: in the puppet film the puppet who originally presented the others with the bricks does join in the subsequent argument, saying they are still the same, and it is possible that the children identified with her as the experimenter and therefore supported her point of view. However, once again, the significance of the context has been underlined.

There have been a number of studies which claim to show that young children demonstrate an understanding of conservation under certain circumstances. One of the earliest of these was Frank's screening experiment (reported in Bruner, 1966a, p. 193), in which a screen was placed between the child and the experimenter so that the child could not see the transformation or its results. In these circumstances children appear to expect the quantity to remain unchanged. Piaget (Piaget and Inhelder, 1963b/ 1969) argued that when he carried out a screening experiment the children stated that the liquid level in the new container would be the same as it had been in the original one. Thus he called the children 'pseudo-conservers' since they were merely assuming that nothing had changed as the result of the transformation thus showing a lack of understanding of either that as the shape of the jar changed the liquid level would change, or that, for example, increased height would be compensated for by decreased width.

Miller and Heldmeyer (1975), having reviewed Frank's and Piaget's experiments, considered whether the number and type of perceptual cues would influence the child's behaviour. After a verbal pre-test of 'more', 'less' and 'same' the children were divided into three groups. The first had a standard conservation test, while the second was given fewer perceptual cues in that the transformation was screened but the child was shown an identical, empty container and told it was 'the same as the one behind the screen'. In the third condition, after the child had responded to the empty-glass question and the transformation had taken place behind the screen, the screen was removed. The results showed that while the 5-year-olds were affected by the amount of perceptual information, the 6-year-olds were not. Their findings were particularly relevant as a contrast to Piaget's since:

> Both kindergartners and first graders gave a high proportion of conservation judgements *with logical explanations* on the first presentation of the completely screened transformation. . . . All but one of these logical explanations were of the 'previous equality' or 'addition-subtraction' type. Thus, the belief in invariance was not simply based on a belief that the container behind the screen had the same water level as the visible container. (Miller and Heldmeyer, 1975, p. 591)

They concluded that the youngest children would display an understanding of invariance under the most facilitating conditions, and thus 'the conservation of liquid quantity is not an all-or-none ability' (p. 591).

Bryant (1974) has argued, on the basis of his experimental evidence, that the thought of the young child is characterized by a preference for relative as opposed to absolute values, which results in their being unduly dependent on external frames of reference which 'they use inferentially in order to remember and learn from their perceptual encounters with the environment' (p. 13). He believes that it is this characteristic which underlies the results found from many seemingly different types of experiment, for example into children's understanding of absolute and relative learning, of transitive inferences and of conservation. With reference to conservation of number he sees the child as initially using either one-to-one correspondence or length as a means of assessing the relative length of the two rows of counters without being aware that one is a better method than the other of judging number. Therefore, if in the conservation task children initially use one-to-one correspondence to judge whether the rows are equal, in the transformation, when the counters are spaced out, they may use the length cue, not because they believe that the number of counters has changed but because they believe that their first judgement was incorrect. He tested this by, first of all, showing the children three static displays of counters and asking them to choose the most numerous row in each display. They were consistently correct with A, as they used one-to-one

Figure 1 Visual displays of counters

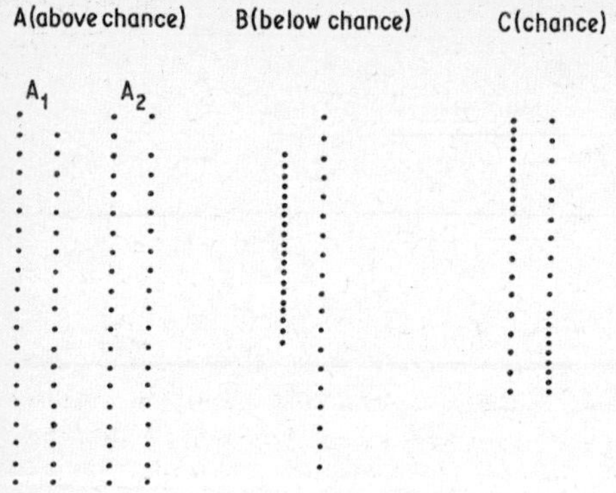

Source: Bryant, 1974, p. 116.

correspondence, and incorrect with B, using length, and used chance with C since neither the length nor the one-to-one-correspondence cue was available. He then transformed the A display first to a B display and second to a C display. He found that the children were then above chance in their choices in the C display since they had transferred their correct judgement, using one-to-one correspondence, from A to C, but were incorrect with B since the two judgements, of length and one-to-one correspondence, conflicted.

The conditions which cause variations in a child's performance are, intrinsically, interesting in that they can help reveal the mental processes of the child. Thus the role of the context of the task, or the non-structural features of the task, are crucial. Miller (1979) argued that concepts develop over time from an initial stage, when, for example, the child will exhibit an understanding of invariance in certain contexts, to the final stage, when the fully developed concept is applied in all relevant situations, and that this developmental process should therefore be studied by asking

'*In what sense* (e.g. under what attentional and memory conditions) does the child conserve?' (p. 155). This seems an eminently sensible approach and one which makes positive use of the studies reviewed here, rather than seeing them mainly as disconfirmations of the Piagetian position. Disconfirmations are of little value if they do not offer a comparable alternative theory which can be tested by means which are independent of both previous theories.

It is possible that a study of the conditions which affect the young child's performance would complement Piaget's work on some aspects of thinking underlying that performance. The use of what appear to be irrelevant contextual cues, and which indeed, at the time, lead to an illogical performance, may if seen as part of the whole process of development, form an extremely positive stage. Thus this period of contextual sensitivity may be a prior condition for operativity with a positive value of its own rather than just being a form of thinking which has to be overcome, or put right, by operativity. Just as children need their milk teeth, although they drop out as the second teeth develop, so too they may need this period of prelogical, pre-operational thinking.

Perception

We have seen that the young child lives in a perceptually dominated world but to believe that the child perceives as the adult perceives may be as misleading as believing that the child thinks as the adult thinks. At the simplest level children do not seem to scan objects systematically, as adults do, but rather attend to particularly salient features. Braine (1972) found that children below the age of 5 initially notice an outstanding feature and then scan downwards from there; whereas older children start at the top and scan downwards. There is, however, more to visual perception than scanning, since it implies not just seeing but categorizing what has been seen. Hence the distinction between perception and cognition is not absolute. The early years in school require children to use their perceptual powers more self-consciously so as to pay attention to the orientation of lines as a basis for reading, or to realize that a two-dimensional picture can represent a three-dimensional object. In other words the child now has to learn to perceive symbols as well as objects. Children as young as 2 years appear to have little difficulty in recognizing realistic pictures of objects (Hochberg and Brooks, 1962), although they have more difficulty with non-realistic representation (Elkind, 1970). Increasing age enables them to integrate the information they are receiving more easily and to use it more efficiently.

Many years ago Kepes (1945) argued that perceiving a picture is analogous to understanding a language in that it involves both semantics, i.e. the meaning assigned to the arbitrary visual configuration, and syntax, or the artistic conventions employed in a particular picture. On the other hand Gibson (1969) held that pictures act as 'surrogates' for real-world perceptions by giving the same equivalent to the eye or brain as did the original. Support for the latter view is given by the fact that young children find realistic pictures easier to recognize since they more directly mirror what the child sees. Even infants appear to be able to distinguish between objects and pictures of objects, as shown by Younas (1973) who habituated seven 18-week-old infants to either a bump or a depression on a flat surface. The infants were then shown photographs of the bump or the depression and they looked longer at the novel object, suggesting that the photograph was recognized as a representation of the bump or the depression. Fagan (1972) then showed that the ability to recognize line drawings as representing faces comes later than the ability to recognize photographs.

Obviously if pictures use an *arbitrary* symbolic system to portray events in the world, such as, for example, using stylized means of representing movement in a picture of road signs, then children will not be able to decode the symbolic system and may well interpret, for example, the sign for men working on a road as a man opening an umbrella. Not until approximately the age of 10 are children able to perceive the properties of pictures themselves, i.e. children younger than this cannot concentrate on the *medium* itself but remain centrated on the object signified (Gardner, 1970, 1972a, 1972b). Thus if they are first shown paintings by Renoir and then asked to pick a Renoir out of a second group of paintings they cannot use his style as a touchstone but rather choose a Picasso because its subject matter matches one of the pictures in the first group. This may be an example of a wider phenomenon of child thought namely their inability to focus on *ways* of thinking, speaking or perceiving. They do not distinguish between the process and the content conveyed by the process, a distinction which is crucial for success in educational tasks (see p. 114).

When young children are asked to learn to read, the phonetic alphabet makes the perceptual task considerably more complex than that of perceiving pictures. Initially children need to realize that words are made up of simple letters and that the order of letters in each word is not arbitrary, nor indeed is the order of the words themselves. Four-year-olds have been found to be able to distinguish letters from other stimuli such as drawings and scribbles (Lavine, cited in Gibson, 1970). Seven-year-olds used certain distinguishing features to discriminate between types of letters, and this became more subtle with age so that an initial distinction between straight and curved letters would be followed by differentiations within each set into round and looped curves, and into line orientations in straight letters. Once letters are combined into words children need to perceive the word as a unit, not as a string of letters, and also to realize that the spaces mark the beginnings and ends of units. The child, having seen two initial letters, and perhaps the configuration of the word as a whole, is thought to set up a hypothesis as to what the word is and then check it out by scanning other letters. It is at this stage that the meaning of words and words in sentences adds to the child's ability to check his or her hypothesis, and reading moves beyond perception.

Memory

During the early years in school there is further development in children's memory. As they gain increasing knowledge of the world so they are able to order the objects to be remembered into the relevant categories and hence remember better. De Groot (1979) and Chase and Simon (1973) showed that the ability to recall the position of pieces on a chess board depends on the person's knowledge and skill at chess. Chi (1978) found that children who were skilled chess-players remembered the positions better than adults who were not, which would suggest that age is less important than having the relevant knowledge of the material to be remembered. By the age of 6 to 7 children appear to be able to remember the salient features of prose passages as well as adults do. They then become able to make inferences from the material

97

in the passage and use these in their memorizing (Paris and Lindauer, 1976), so that by 11 or 12 they will infer the presence of an oven if a person is described baking a cake and use this in their memory of the passage, showing how their increasing knowledge of actions and their implications, aids representation and hence memory.

Between the ages of 6 and 8 children become aware that memory can be observed in themselves and that means can be taken to improve it. They have knowledge of memory or 'metamemory'. Of this Flavell (1977) asks the important question, 'If metamemory is knowledge of memory what might such knowledge include?' (p. 209). He saw it as having three components: first, *sensitivity*, which enables the child to realize that memory can be deliberately improved and is not just something that happens. For example, Masur *et al.* (1973) asked 6-year-olds, 8-year-olds and adults to remember a set of pictures. After their first attempt they were told they could study the pictures and then try again. While the 8-year-olds and the adults concentrated on the pictures they had failed to remember, the 6-year-olds looked equally at both those with which they had failed and those with which they had succeeded. Secondly, Flavell distinguished between *knowledge of memory in general and knowledge of one's own memory abilities*. Young children were found to over-estimate their memory abilities in comparison with older children (Flavell and Wellman, 1977), and the older ones were also better at knowing when they had learned material well enough to be able to recall it accurately. Thirdly, children gradually learn that memorizing is *more difficult in some situations* than others.

While memory is important in education it seems that the process of schooling may itself facilitate memory development, at least in those cultures in which the demands of the school and the demands of the general culture are significantly different (see p. 120). Wagner (1973) studied the effect of schooling and urban environment on memory in Morocco. He found that both led to better short-term memory for pictures, with the effect of the school becoming more noticeable as the children got older, possibly because they developed the strategy of rehearsal. However, Kagan *et al.* (1979) carried out a cross-cultural study of recall memory in two Guatemalan towns and one American city and found that schooling did not seem to be critical, for improved strategies for recall appeared in all the children at about the age of 9 or 10. In considering their findings the authors make a point which is highly relevant for children in the early years of school:

> The data also implied that an important psychological change emerges around 9–10 years of age . . . the growth of an expectation that, if one attempts to generate knowledge and strategies in an initially difficult problem situation, performance will be enhanced. . . . Although American children become more reflective in problem situations at ages 5 and 6 and start to use rehearsal to aid recall, they usually do not behave as if they believe that an unfamiliar problem has a rule or principle which, if detected, will permit solution. (Kagan *et al.*, 1979, pp. 60–1)

It is precisely this form of metacognition which the school requires of the child, and its presence may distinguish between those who are and those who are not ready to take part in the intentional transmission of knowledge and skills which informs the activities of school.

Social interaction and cognitive development

When children enter school, in addition to being faced with a range of new tasks and being required to develop an awareness of their own mental processes and strategies for learning, they will also find themselves a member of a group of peers. As well as having social influence, peers may also facilitate cognitive development by presenting a child with alternative points of view which cause the child to restructure his or her own (Piaget, 1924/1926). Lloyd and Burgess (1974) tested Piaget's hypothesis by carrying out a detailed analysis of the cognitive changes which occurred when children of different levels of cognitive maturity were working on a class-inclusion task as a group. To investigate this, sixteen groups were formed consisting of three girls each, aged 6 years to 6 years 11 months. Some groups were composed of children with the same level of cognitive maturity, as assessed on a pre-test, and some had children of mixed level, i.e. in Piaget's terms some were operational and some were pre-operational. Each group was then asked to work together on a constrained card or object-sorting task, to agree an answer and to report their agreed group solution to the experimenter. During the sorting tasks the experimenter was not present but children were video-taped through a two-way mirror. At the end of the final session the children were individually post-tested. The control children did a pre- and post-test but did not take part in any group sessions. The results of the analysis of the video-tape and the differences in the pre-test and post-test scores showed that group experience could improve performance and that mixed-ability grouping did not lower the attainment of the more mature children, but that the more mature affected the thinking of the less mature only if the more mature were also socially dominant, i.e. who the child was was as important as what she said or did.

Miller and Brownell (1975) also looked at social/cognitive dominance and found that while on conservation questions the conservers won 59 arguments and the non-conservers 8, on other questions the figures were 41 and 38 respectively, suggesting that generally these conservers, whether dominant or not, could still win arguments when they were in possession of the more mature understanding. It could, however, be the case that change in the non-conservers' post-test behaviour will be affected both by losing the argument and by whom they lost it to.

Perret-Clermont (1980) carried out a series of experiments into the effects of social interaction on cognitive development and argued that its facilitating effects could not be attributed to mere imitation of a more advanced model. The effects seemed to be due to the fact that the mature model stimulated the more immature thinker to restructure, rather than providing a ready-made way of thinking. If the difference between the two was too large the younger child would not see the incompatibility between his or her view and the model's and hence, seeing no problem, would not restructure. If the model was just slightly more advanced, such an incompatibility would, according to this view, be apparent and hence lead to restructuring. Mugny and Doise (1978) pre-tested children on spatial relations and then divided them into pairs for their experiment which involved their working together. The least mature children did not compensate (NC) for changes in the frame of reference, the most mature compensated fully (FC) and an intermediate group made partial compensations (PC). The question at issue was the effect on performance of various com-binations of pairs. NC children did not benefit from being with another NC or with an FC but did benefit when paired with a PC. PCs benefited when paired with each other or with FCs. However, some PCs benefited from an NC partner, suggesting that progression can result merely by exposure to a different viewpoint, not necessarily a more mature one.

Russell (1979) has argued that conflict is not in itself sufficient. The child also needs to hear the correct answer, and reasons for it, rather than just being exposed to another form of non-conservation. Glachen and Light (1982) tested children to see whether peer interaction rather than individual experience would improve children's performance on the tower of Hanoi problem which requires the child to move unequal sized discs stacked on one stick to another stick in such a way that a larger disc is never on top of a smaller one, making use of a third stick as an intermediate step. They found that exposure to conflicting viewpoints was not sufficient, in that if a dominant child solved the problem his or her partner improved little, but if there were joint decisions so that the majority of moves were determined by both children, then there was an improvement in performance between the pre-test and the post-test.

School readiness

Since the ages 5–7 do seem to span a significant transitional period, it follows that individual children, of the same chronological age, will be at different stages in this cognitive progression. This has the unfortunate consequence that though some 5-year-olds are more able, cognitively, than others to respond to the demands of school, the time of school entry is determined simply by chronological age. Neither mental age nor emotional maturity are taken into account. Given this, reception-class teachers have to cater for a wide range not of potential ability, necessarily, but of actual maturity.

Hall and Kaye (1980) studied the cognitive development of four sub-cultural groups (black and white, lower- and middle-class boys) between the ages of 6 and 9. The usual effects of race and class were found but they also found that although the black and lower-class children were behind at age 6 they improved at more or less the same rate as the middle-class children till age 9 but were of course still behind then because of their initial lag. The authors do not believe there is any inherent difference in the abilities of the groups, simply that the white middle-class groups are ready for school at an earlier chronological age. They suggest that

> training too early can result in poor achievement and negative affect toward both school and subject matter. Waiting until a child is ready or even until after a child is ready will result in much more success and positive affect. (Hall and Kaye, 1980, pp. 61–2)

In her commentary published with this research Scarr argued:

> In the light of these facts I would like to suggest a radical solution; that black and lower class children be given intensive training on basic skills of literacy and numeracy from kindergarten on, even if they do not get any training in music, art, or recreational sport . . . the reality is that culturally and socially disadvantaged children cannot wait until they are optimally ready to learn school skills. Unless someone can demonstrate that they can catch up later if instruction begins later, then I think their instruction will have to begin ready or not. (pp. 82–3).

There is a third alternative. The work of constructivists such as Piaget would indicate that, for example, one cannot expect children to carry out tasks requiring a developed concept of number unless they have previously developed the ability to classify, seriate and conserve; nor will practice with number tasks necessarily aid this development. However, merely to wait until children are ready does not seem sensible if becoming ready requires them to be involved in the very types of experience which enable them to develop these concepts. What is required is a two-pronged attack, first by exposure to the forms of experience thought to give rise to the basic categories of human understanding, which are themselves a precondition for subsequent learning; and secondly by alerting children to the nature of learning tasks in school.

There is a growing awareness that successful learning requires children both to understand what 'learning' is and to be able to select the most appropriate strategies for learning a particular content. Before coming to school it is most likely that children will have been exposed to real-life trial-and-error learning when, for example, they try to learn to ride a bicycle or to swim and, if asked, would probably say one learns to ride a bicycle by getting on it and trying. They will also have learned certain procedures, such as unlocking a door or laying the table, by watching adults and copying them. School-learning, however, is different in kind in that it requires children to realize that their own mind is the means they must employ in order to manipulate symbols which represent the world in various ways. This is known as 'knowing about knowing', or 'metacognition'. Even in their first school, the educational system requires children to reflect upon their own cognitive processes so that, for example, they become aware of memory as a process under the control of the person memorizing. This ability to be self-regarding may well be facilitated by adults who enable children to develop role-taking abilities by taking their view overtly into account and alerting them to the fact that they have a point of view and that it can be considered both by themselves and by others as an object of cognition.

When faced with many cognitive tasks children below the age of 8 or 9 do not make plans to help themselves or understand strategies of study. Not till 11 or 12 can they abstract the salient points from a piece of continuous prose, or the central point of a story, and hence store such information for use as an *aide-mémoire* (Brown and Smiley, 1977; Danner, 1976). Forrest and Waller (1979) found that young children and poor readers could not adjust their reading strategies when asked to 'study' a passage, 'skim' it or read it just for enjoyment. Another problem is that young children are not good listeners and do not ask questions if they do not understand. Karabenick and Miller (1977) found that 60 per cent of inadequate messages were accepted by the 5-, 6- and 7-year-olds in their study. However, if they are shown *how* to ask questions when they are unclear, their performance will improve (Cosgrove and Patterson, 1977).

In order to learn to read, a crucial first-school task, the child must first realize what it means to read, i.e. that meaningful information can be abstracted from the marks on the page. Reid (1966) found that some children did not realize why their parents held a newspaper in front of them or how the postman used the written address to find out to whom to deliver letters. Younger and poorer readers were found by Golinkoff (1976) to concentrate on single words in a passage, and not on the meaning of the words in the passage, nor on the meaning of the passage as a whole; nor did they correct their mistakes, suggesting that for them 'reading' was little more than a mechanical decoding. They may not have made the crucial link between meaning and the printed word, a link which they made with the spoken word while still in infancy. Between the ages of 8 and 12 there is considerable improvement in reading for meaning, learning how to skim a passage and adjusting strategies in response to different reading requirements.

The implication of the above findings is that children's scholastic skills may be improved by deliberate training in metacognitive activities, whether for memory tasks (Brown, 1978), listening (Cosgrove and Patterson, 1977) or reading (Stauffer, 1969), rather than by increased practice in the activities themselves. On the other hand, skill in numeracy tasks or tasks based on other basic concepts may be more easily facilitated, not only by a meta-analysis of their components, but also by exposing the child to the types of experience which are a precondition for the development of such concepts.

5

Middle school (8–13)

Operational thinking – Piaget's approach

As children enter middle school their cognition will be characterized by the development of what Piaget called 'concrete operations'. The idea of an 'operation' is central to Piaget's constructivism, and the characteristics of child thought at this age cannot be understood if the concrete-operational stage is thought of as little more than the period when children resolve the difficulties they had in the pre-operational stage. It is true that at this stage the child becomes able to comprehend the nature of classes, to perceive the spatio-temporal relationship between objects and their constituent parts and to grasp the properties of measurement and arithmetic groups. However, the important question is, 'What kind of cognitive structure must be presupposed in order for a child to be able to carry out such cognitive tasks successfully?' Piaget's view was that as development takes place the early schemes, based on overt actions, are transformed into the schemes of internalized actions or 'operations'. By an 'operation'

Piaget meant that the overt actions of the sensori-motor period were internalized so that the child could represent an action mentally and thereby run through an action sequence in his or her mind without having to act it out. The value of this was that once operations developed the child could, mentally, reverse actions, and the reversibility of operations is one of their distinguishing characteristics. Just as the infant combined single actions into schemes, so the concrete-operational child was thought to combine the internalized actions (operations) into organized systems of thought. Hence an operation must always be part of an organized structure. Piaget and Inhelder (1963a/1969) believed that such operational groupings had a distinct logical structure:

> Underlying language and at a level far below conscious reflection, there exists a logic of co-ordination of actions, if one rates as logical the relations of order, inclusion, etc., which regulate actions as they are later to regulate thought. The notion of operation is thus psychologically natural. This is so not only if one calls by that name internalised actions (uniting, dissociating, ordering, etc.) which can be performed in both directions (reversibility) but also if one characterises internalised actions by their most specific genetic property which is that they are abstracted from the most general co-ordination of actions. Operations are thus only a higher form of regulations, and that is enough to guarantee their psychological authenticity. . . . The second fundamental characteristic of operations, which follows directly from the first, is that they are always structured in integrated systems. (Piaget and Inhelder, 1963a/1969, vol. 7, pp. 154–5)

Piaget saw this structure as capable of being modelled by the nine '*groupements*', or quasi-logical/mathematical groupings, of classes and relations.

1 *Primary addition of classes:* this grouping models the child's ability to compose and decompose hierarchies of classes. Any class A, while forming the superordinate class which includes all the subordinates below it, is in turn a sub-class of another superordinate, for example the class of dogs, which includes all breeds, is a sub-class of canines and equivalent to wolves. Inhelder and Piaget (1959/1964) studied this grouping with reference to class inclusion, and found that the pre-operational child was

unable to combine and recombine the subordinate classes, or understand the necessary reversibility whereby if $A + B = C$ then $C - B = A$.

2 *Secondary addition of classes:* this also relates to hierarchies of classes but of the kind in which if, for example, the class under consideration is flowers (class F) then it can be thought of as being composed of two or more equivalent sub-classes, for example roses (class g) plus all other species of flower (g^1) so that $g + g^1 = F$. However, F could be seen to consist of chrysanthemums (H) plus all other species of flower (H_1) and then class g would have become part of (H_1). This cognitive structure enables the child to realize that objects can be classified in more than one way and that the different groupings are equivalent.

For example, when Inhelder and Piaget (1959/1964) asked children to classify 4 blue circles, 4 blue squares, 4 red circles and 4 red squares, only operational children could classify by colour and then rearrange the classification and use shape.

3 *Bi-univocal multiplication of classes:* the understanding modelled here is the multiplication of classes leading to the realization that an element can be a member of two classes at one and the same time. If, for example, one wishes to apply the categories of men/women/middle class/working class to a given group one can first divide the group into two (men and women) and then subdivide these into middle class and working class. If one then recombines these elements, four possible categories are formed, namely middle-class men, middle-class women, working-class men, working-class women. There is thus a one-to-one correspondence between the sub-sections, i.e. there is no case of a man being neither working class nor middle class, given this categorization. It is also the basis of understanding the intersection of classes so that for a person to be placed in a particular category she, for example, must be *both* working-class and female.

4 *Co-univocal multiplication of classes:* this is like (3) except that the multiplication is between one member of one series and several members of another, as in kinship tables. For example John and Robert can both be Florence's grandsons. However, John is also Peter's brother and Robert's cousin, while Robert is John's and Peter's cousin but Jane's brother.

The final four groupings show Piaget's belief that the groupings modelled an individual's understanding not of classes of objects, but of relationships between objects.

5 *Addition of asymmetrical relations:* this models the understanding of the relationship 'bigger than'/'smaller than', such that if B is bigger than A and smaller than C, then C must be bigger than A. This grouping underlies the ability to seriate and to realize that height, etc., is relative to what goes before and after.

In another context, this grouping models the understanding that Matthew can be both the father of Mark and a son of Luke.

6 *Addition of symmetrical relationships:* here, if A is the same height as B, then B must be the same height as A, and if John is Paul's brother, then Paul must be John's brother. This understanding also aids the child in working out what is not the case, so that if Jane is not John's sister then she is not Paul's sister either. Pre-operation children often have difficulty in understanding that if French children are foreigners to British children then the latter are also foreigners to the former. Similarly if a child, Jane, knows she has a sister Jill she may not accept that Jill has a sister called Jane.

7 *Bi-univocal multiplication of relations:* this grouping models the realization that, for example, blue flowers in a border can vary from light-blue to dark-blue in colour and from short to tall in height. Once children realize this, they can form a matrix ranging from the shortest, lightest flowers to the tallest, darkest ones and fit any flower into its proper position.

8 *Co-univocal multiplication of relations:* this models the fourth group of classes. The multiplication is of one relationship to more than one in the other set, not just on the single dimension of, for example, lighter/darker, shorter/taller, as in (7). So that, to use Flavell's (1963) kinship example, this grouping enables the child to work out that 'if A is the father of B, and B is the first cousin of C, then A is the father of the first cousin of C and thus the uncle of C' (p. 186).

9 *The preliminary grouping of equalities:* this last grouping involves 'pure equivalence' so that if A = B and B = C, then A must equal C.

There is an old puzzle which defeats pre-operational children simply because they cannot deal with hierarchies of classes, nor relationships between classes. The child is told that a person looks at a photograph and says 'Brothers and sisters have I none but this man's father is my father's son'. The child has to say whose photograph the person is holding. There is no difficulty here except in structuring the problem, and it is the ability to structure problems of this kind which, according to Piaget, is absent before the appearance of operatory thinking. He believed that if the internalized actions of the concrete operational period were structured the properties of such structures were important, and that when faced with a problem the operational child took the approach that was most clearly explained by positing structures having the form of the *groupements* or, at least, by hypothesizing that such cognitive structures are logically possible.

Piaget (1955/1958) also maintained that the stage of concrete operational thinking was characterized by a sense of purpose in the child, showing an ability to think about thinking:

> concrete operations are actions accompanied by an awareness on the part of the subject of the techniques and co-ordinations of his own behaviour, these characteristics distinguishing operations from simple goal directed behaviour, and they are precisely those characteristics not found when the subject acts only with a view toward achieving a goal; he does not ask himself why he succeeds. (p. 6)

'*Concrete*' operations meant for Piaget that the child could only apply this form of thinking to real-world objects and events. The ability to think of possible events, to develop hypotheses and to apply operations to operations, i.e. to consider thought processes operationally, was for Piaget the achievement of the stage of '*formal*' operations.

When studying children at this age his approach was to test the children and see if this cognitive performance suggested that they were using cognitive structures which could be modelled by the *groupements*. He did not gather his empirical evidence first and then realize that what he saw could be modelled in that way: rather he began with the model of the structures and used his experiments to see if they existed. For Piaget a prime characteristic of operational thought was that it is reversible and he saw the ability to conserve as marking the boundary between pre-operational and operational thinking (Piaget and Inhelder, 1963a/1969):

The best criterion for the emergence of operations at the level of concrete structures (toward the age of 7) is, in fact, the constitution of invariants or notions of conservation. Observation shows, as we shall see from several examples, that a child who can internalise an action or imagine its result is not necessarily able to visualise *ipso facto* the possibility of performing the same action in reverse and thus cancelling the result. In other words, an action does not at once transform itself into a reversible operation. There are a number of intermediaries such as imagining reversal, but on request or as a new action distinct from the first and not implied by it (this we shall call 'empirical reversal'). It is therefore not easy to recognise in the subject the beginnings of reversibility as such, except by its results. Yet, one has only to listen to what the subject says once he has mastered the notion of reversibility, to obtain an expression of reversibility and consequently of operations (internalised actions that have become reversible) which is remarkably simple and exact. Moreover, it coincides with the best of logical definitions: an operation is that which transforms a state A into a state B leaving at least one property invariant throughout the transformation and allowing the possibility of return from B to A thereby cancelling the transformation. It so happens – and this time diagnosis is easy – that at pre-operational levels the transformation is conceived as modifying all the data at once, without any conservation. This of course makes it impossible to return to the point of departure without a new action transforming the whole once more (re-creating what has been destroyed etc.) and consequently differing from the first instead of remaining the same action but inversed. That is why we feel that tests dealing with conservation give the best indication of the natural, and not merely the logical, reality of operations. (p. 156)

Alternatives to Piaget

Piaget's description of child thought during this period has been challenged both generally and in particular. Sheppard (1978a, 1978b) argued that Piaget's notion of relating child thought to the mathematical group had value:

It emphasises structure of thought. Thought is not seen to be made of isolated units, but as forming wholes. It conforms to a system of interrelationships, of intertwinings, and of inter-dependencies, this system being a combinatorial one, at the heart of which is the operation on the elements of the system. (p. 53)

However, as Sheppard pointed out, Piaget's formulation of group properties has been criticized by both mathematicians (Witz, 1969) and logicians (Grize, 1960). He therefore proposed the 'groupoid' as a more appropriate model for child thought. It involves first the combination of elements, and secondly mapping, or assigning elements to other elements, e.g. the series 2, 4, 6, can be mapped to 4, 16, 36, by the operation of squaring. For Sheppard the ability to combine and map is the defining characteristic of operational thought. He saw it as involving the ability to consider two sets of elements, e.g. roses and tulips, and then a third set, 'flowers', of which both roses and tulips are part and to which both contribute but which is not the actual set before the child, as it would be if, for example, flowers were being considered beside grasses as subjects of a larger set.

A more basic criticism comes from those who do not believe that thinking is 'structured' at all and therefore do not accept that the disparate task successes of this period reflect any *general* cognitive change. Rather each task is seen as consisting in a series of sub-skills and successful learning requires that these discrete sub-skills be learned but does not imply any form of cognitive restructuring. The fact that the child is able to exhibit thinking of a certain level on some tasks and not others (the child will conserve substance earlier than weight, and weight earlier than volume), gives some support to their view. It is difficult to see why a child who can operationally conserve cannot conserve in all contexts. More recently Piaget (1970b) argued that development should be seen as a spiral rather than a series of steps and therefore the child's cognitive structures do not have to change totally. Never-theless this does not entirely explain why a single structure should be differentially applied depending on the characteristics of the task. It implies a much greater degree of dialectical relationship between the characteristic of the task, its elements and the thinking subject than Piaget usually allows for.

Furby (1980) maintained that while cross-cultural research had highlighted the role of the environment in cognitive development, the environment itself had never been given the detailed analysis which the human thinker had received, nor had the relationship between specific environments and specific tasks been spelled out. She quotes Fischer's theory (1980) to the effect that cognitive development is the development of specific skills which are essentially affected by the environmental context. That is, the organism's control of a skill is dependent on a particular environmental context. Thus differences in performance on tasks would imply not general differences in cognitive structures but specific differences in organism/environment interaction. The analysis of tasks and the skills required to carry them out successfully becomes as important as an analysis of the characteristics of the thinking of the person engaged on such tasks. This she feels will lead to 'an increasing interest in the *process* of development (i.e. the transformation of one skill with another) rather than the products of development (i.e. stages)' (p. 559).

There are therefore two broad approaches to thinking at this age. The one sees a qualitative change in thinking resulting from the development of 'operational' thought in its concrete form, and the other sees it as the development of skills of increasing sophistication. However, since in many countries children of this age are in school, two related questions are, first, the degree to which cognitive development is affected by schooling and, secondly, the extent to which theories of cognitive development and research findings can affect schooling via the curriculum.

The significance of schooling for cognitive development

An argument running through much cross-cultural research takes the form 'that people who go to school for a number of years and acquire literacy and numeracy, are likely to think in rather different ways from those who have never had this experience' (Hallpike, 1976, p. 263). Greenfield (1966) studied schooled and unschooled Senegalese Wolof children's understanding of the conservation of quantity. The children were divided into groups: the first was not attending school and lived in a rural area; the second lived in the same rural area and attended a local school; and the third attended school and lived in an urban setting. What she found was that only half the rural unschooled children were able to conserve by the age of 11 to 13 whereas both the urban and rural school children had attained conservation by then. Her explanation was that schooling caused the children, first, to attend to the perceptual change and then to move on to conservation, whereas the unschooled children gave less perceptual reasons initially and, once these increased, did not overcome the perceptual saliency. The unschooled children were much more likely to say that the amount had changed because the experimenter had poured it, a response Greenfield calls 'magical'. However, if McGarrigle and Donaldson's analysis is correct (see p. 89), it may merely mean that the child has noticed the experimenter's action, given greater weight to it than her words, and hence commented on the action. The schooled children, on the other hand, are able to pay attention to her words and realize that they are being asked about quantity and, indeed, that the whole problem could be posed verbally with no need for experimental materials at all. Similarly Cole and Scribner (1974) studied the Kpelle in Nigeria and argued that schooling, which necessarily involved literacy, caused differences in performance between the schooled and the unschooled. In a second study of the Vai they were able to study a literate and non-literate group, but the literacy of the former was not gained in school, being taught by a friend or relative. Therefore the specific effect of literacy could be distinguished from the more general effect of schooling. They found few differences between the groups except that the literate Vai were more able to explain a board game to another person when the materials were not before them, i.e. they were able to use language independently of any perceptual support.

Stevenson (1982) carried out a detailed study of schooling in Peru in which the influence of additional variables, such as family characteristics and rural as against urban environments, were also assessed since it is possible that children who attend school may come from homes which differ from those of the children who do not attend school, and it is this difference rather than schooling *per se* which results in the schooled children's improved performance on tasks. However, at the end of his study his conclusion was that schooling had a positive effect on performance when all other effects of 'sex, location, parental education, home quality, and parental use of reward' had been accounted for. In contrast Kagan *et al*. (1979), who studied recall memory and conservation in an American city (Cambridge, Massachusetts), a wealthy progressive

Guatemalan town with a good school (San Pedro) and a poorer, more isolated, less literate Guatemalan town (San Marcos), found that recall memory improved at different ages in the different settings (7 to 8 in Cambridge; 8 to 9 in San Pedro, and 10 to 11 in San Marcos) but that the change could not depend on schooling as it occurred in all the children. These researchers also found little correlation between performance on memory and performance on conservation tasks, pointing to the importance of the nature of the specific task set for the child. Schooling is a particular type of experience which gives rise to certain forms of cognitive growth in that it is largely symbolically transmitted, decontextualized learning, which is intended to be non-specific, and hence specific understandings become generalizable to a range of similar problems. To this extent what children learn in school transcends both time and space in that the knowledge transmitted by past and present strangers is presented to them in distinction to the immediate and the personal. Children are thus in the unenviable position of having to learn skills whose relevance is not apparent to them and of having to make their own a form of knowledge, which to begin with is in no sense their own, or part of their experience. However, it may be that the very process of distancing themselves from what they learn is precisely what is required to make them aware of their own thought processes and hence stimulate development. If children are not required to learn material that does not relate to their daily life then the separation of the thinker from the thought-about may not take place. The role of the school in this process is not entirely clear. Children who attend school may never in fact make the above crucial distinction, nor may those who are not schooled necessarily fail to do so. Warren (1980) suggested that 'schooling makes a difference when it is a major source of cultural stimulation of a novel, "modern" kind for a basically non-literate culture' (p. 307), the implication being that:

Western culture [has] been brought – probably in large part by the institution of universal schooling, not so long ago – to a general level of stimulation of its young which ironically lessens the direct differential effect of formal schooling on cognitive growth. (p. 307)

Given, in western culture, the enormous disparity of what is offered to children under the umbrella term 'schooling', which is compounded by the individual differences that affect what children can get out of what is offered, it becomes difficult to see any overall commonality in the experience of 'schooling', although there will be similarity of experience amongst groups *within* the total population. It is with these in mind that we now turn to the relevance of cognitive theory and research findings for the school curriculum.

The application of theory to practice

Piaget seldom attempted to apply his theory to educational practice beyond general maxims of the kind 'we really possess only what we have conquered for ourselves' or 'It is idle . . . to try to transform the child's mind from outside when his own taste for active research and his desire for co-operation suffice to ensure normal intellectual development' (1932, p. 392). Clearly there is no need to attempt to accelerate the developmental milestones outlined by Piaget. Children attain them spontaneously, without direct teaching. While Piaget's description of the process of equilibration may be relevant for the learning of certain concepts, especially those numerical and scientific notions of particular interest to him, its *direct* application to the learning of reading or writing, for example, is less clear.

Ginsberg (1981) was largely sceptical of the contribution of Piaget to education, believing that his interest in the development of the basic categories of human understanding left him with 'little to say about the acquisition and nature of culturally-based forms of knowledge, the forms inculcated by schooling' (p. 329). However, he did point out that Piaget's suggestion that the child's intuitive understanding should be harnessed for school subjects was a 'key idea for education' (p. 326). He quotes Piaget's view that

> it is difficult to conceive how students who are well endowed when it comes to elaboration and utilization of the spontaneous logicomathematical structures of intelligence can find themselves handicapped in the comprehension of a branch of teaching that bears exclusively upon what is to be derived from such structures. (Piaget, 1970a, p. 44)

He also quotes Piaget's belief that

> the pedagogic problem . . . still subsists in its entirety: that of

finding the most adequate methods for bridging the transition between these natural but non-reflective structures ... to conscious reflection upon such structures and to a theoretical formulation of them. (Piaget, 1970a, p. 47)

Ginsberg's comment on this was 'There is thus a particularly Piagetian form of consciousness raising: in presenting formalisations, the teacher must make an effort to exploit the child's intuitions' (Ginsburg, 1981, p. 326). This interpretation raises yet again the topic of metacognition. It may be that Piagetian theory will make its greatest contribution by indicating how children can be aided to think about thinking, especially their own, and hence bring under their conscious control strategies which, though already in existence, are not accessible to the child. What is not clear is how this process would help create new structures or strategies, unless the realization that present strategies were inadequate can lead to a greater receptivity either to direct instruction or observational learning.

There have, however, been attempts to relate Piagetian theory to education. Collis (1975) delimited the minimal criteria for distinguishing the thinking of children characterized by one or other of Piaget's stages, the one difference being that the concrete period was extended to cover the early formal stage:

1. *Preoperational.* A response based upon a lack of comprehension; tautology, an irrelevant association, or denial of the data.
2. *Early concrete.* One relevant point is seen but others are missed.
3. *Middle concrete.* Several relevant points are noted but in isolation.
4. *Concrete generalisation.* The relevant dimensions of the data are perceived and their inter-relationship. The response is, however, still tied to the immediate content, as is the case in the preceding level.
5. *Formal.* A superordinate, abstract principle is brought in to enable valid generalisations from the given, with extensions to novel data. There is reluctance to close on a unique answer. (p. 597)

Biggs (1980) then distinguished between the Piagetian 'Hypothetical Cognitive Structure' (HCS) and the 'Structure of Observed

Learning Outcomes' (SOLO), which, like skills, are task specific. This approach saw the teacher as being more concerned with the latter and argued that the SOLO model may be of use to teachers by providing a 'technological', i.e. overt and operational, version of Piagetian theory. Between the stage of cognitive development and the child's response to specific tasks Collis and Biggs interposed the idea of 'working memory space' which refers to 'the amount of space that is available for keeping the relevant elements and operations in the forefront of the "mind's eye" while doing the necessary work to give a response' (Collis, 1980, p. 642). As lower-level operations become more automatic the child has space for the higher-level operations. With respect to mathematics a concrete level of operation will mean that the child will be successful if he or she can work with single operations on concrete elements. Children will realize that $3 + 2 = 5$ and $4 + 1 = 5$ but not that $3 + 2 = 4 + 1$. Later in the period they will still need to arrive at 'closure', i.e. a definite answer, but will accept that $3 + 2 = 4 + 1$ but not, given the larger numbers, that $789 + 326 = 790 + 325$. At the end of the concrete period, children were thought to reach the relational level and to be able to construct more elaborate systems. They were, however, still limited in requiring closure. Children's failure to operate at a certain level, despite their capacity to do so, was attributed to lack of experience and therefore, Collis argued, there is a need to match teaching to their experience in the area until some lower operations become automatic, as well as to relate it to their operational capacity. He relates the model to the school learning of mathematics, giving detailed examples of problems which are appropriate for children at various operatory levels and following the maxim that

> each movement along the continuum from pre-operational to formal operational reasoning, in the case of all the concepts considered, involves being able to cope with increasingly abstract notions so far as elements are concerned and with an increasing complexity of operations on those elements, the two being inextricably linked at all stages of development. (Collis, 1980, p. 670)

There are also a number of studies which indicate that children's understanding of school subjects follows a developmental sequence similar to that which Piagetian theory would predict, e.g.

history (De Silva, 1972; Hallam, 1970; Jurd, 1978a, 1978b), geography (Rhys, 1972), English literature (Mason, 1974), mathematics (Collis, 1976, 1980), science (Shayer *et al.*, 1976, Shayer, 1980). At the pre-operational stage children's approach to the evidence is indiscriminate and they fail to order it in any way. At the concrete level they will use the evidence provided to form a simple hypothesis but will not go beyond the evidence or co-ordinate other points of view. Only at the formal stage will these abilities mature (see p. 122). An obvious implication of these parallels is that curriculum content should approximate to the child's operatory level.

An alternative approach is to draw out the implications of Piagetian theory not for curriculum content but for teaching method. Piaget's prime method of investigating child thought was the 'clinical method'. It was modelled on the methods used in psychoanalytic psychiatric practice which he had used as a young man when interviewing mental patients. He realized (1926/1929) the value of standardized testing but rejected this method, saying that by the form of the question, answers might be suggested to the child and 'the only way to avoid such difficulties is to vary the questions, to make counter suggestions, in short to give up all idea of a fixed questionnaire' (p. 4). He also rejected direct observation:

> therefore even that which could be explained in words, ordinarily remains implicit, simply because the child's thought is not so socialised as our own. But alongside those thoughts which can be expressed, at least internally, how many inexpressible thoughts must remain unknown so long as we restrict ourselves to observing the child without talking to him? . . . The second drawback . . . is the difficulty of distinguishing a child's play from his beliefs. (pp. 6–7)

His solution was to choose a third way which he believed combined the best features of tests and direct observation, namely clinical examination, which he saw as combining experiment and observation with the freedom to question the 'patient' and interpret his or her answers. The latter quality was especially valued by Piaget. He argued that

> it is so hard to find the middle course between systematisation due to preconceived ideas and incoherence due to the absence

of any directing hypothesis.... The experimenter ... must know how to observe, that is to say to let the child talk freely, without ever checking or side-tracking his utterance, and at the same time he must constantly be alert for something definitive, at every moment he must have some working hypothesis, some theory, true or false, which he is seeking to check. (p. 9)

His method has not gone unchallenged. The use of interpretation in the clinical method can mean, as Phillips (1978) pointed out, that Piaget may interpret the child's response as implying the existence of a certain underlying structure when, in fact, there might be several underlying structures which could result in the same response. In a different context Home (1966), criticizing the reification of psychoanalytic concepts, makes a point which is equally applicable to Piaget: 'The lapse in logic occurs when we take an interpretation of behaviour for a description of behaviour – a meaning for a fact' (p. 49).

The purpose of this clinical method was to externalize children's thinking, not to teach them, but it can aid the diagnosis of where cognitive problems may lie and thus enable the teacher to understand the problem. This understanding can then be relayed to children and hence enable them to develop insight into their own thinking. This flexible, diagnostic questioning may be foreign to teachers, who are more inclined to use Socratic questioning, which aims to draw a correct answer out of children, or shape their responses, and hence aid understanding. Both forms of questioning are valuable but they need to be distinguished by the teacher and each used when appropriate.

Other studies have attempted to assess whether the process of learning is indeed affected by the types of experience which Piagetian theory predicts would facilitate cognitive growth. Kuhn (1981) with Ho carried out a study into the mechanisms underlying the transition from concrete to formal thought. The aim was to observe 'the natural development process by means of which individuals construct new reasoning strategies' (p. 354). In this study a pre-test was given to all the children and each experimental child was paired with a matched control. The experimental children were first introduced to the problem and then told to set up any experimental situations they wanted to help them to solve it. With the control children, the experimenter introduced the same problem but then said she would set up some experiments to help them. She then set up the experiment that the control child's matched experimental partner had set up. There was a post-test after the final session and again four months later. The experimentals were found to make either more progress than the controls, or the same; in no pair was the control more advanced. The controls did make some progress as the result of the experience but those who chose what to do did better. The researchers explain their results by saying that the experimental children had to develop an anticipatory scheme as to what they would find out in the experiments they devised and were therefore 'better able to make use of' what came out of the experiments. They concluded that 'the natural process of development of new reasoning strategies involves an individual's attempted reconciling of an observed set of events with a "theory" that he or she has constructed for these events' (p. 357).

Murray (1980) summarized a popular view when he said 'the only certain educational recommendation from a theory such as Piaget's is that schools should simulate "natural" human development . . . schooling . . . promotes intellectual growth best when it is based upon natural mechanisms of human development' (p. 588). This, while being true, may not be the whole truth. The simulation of 'natural' development may be preferable to the inculcation of concepts by verbal means resulting in children's parroting half-understood ideas. However, an 'unnatural' approach which forces the learner to become self-conscious about his or her own learning may also be effective. Intentional instruction in metacognition may form a counterpoint to the incidental, observational learning of everyday life. What results in success or failure in educational practice may not be what is natural or unnatural, spontaneous or intentional, so much as the content to which the unnatural or intentional approach is applied. For example, though forcing children to decode print may have a negative effect on reading ability, it is not clear whether exposure to print and experience of words will, necessarily, be more successful. However, intentionally alerting children to what it means 'to read' and making them consciously aware that they are being asked to acquire a skill may be of most use in helping them to realize that the phonetic code is no more than a conventional vehicle for meaning, like any other code, such as morse or semaphore, and should cause no undue difficulty.

6

Secondary schooling and beyond: adolescence to senescence

Adolescent thought

We have seen that some researchers have argued that concrete thinking requires the child to attend to the meaning of words independent of the context in which they are uttered. Formal thinking, according to Piaget (Inhelder and Piaget, 1955; Piaget, 1972a), requires the adolescent, or young adult, to attend to the *form* of the argument or statement, independent of the content of that statement: hence the term 'formal'. For example, given two mutually exclusive categories, statements of the kind 'The prime minister is either a man or a woman' will always be true, whereas those in the form 'The prime minister is both a man and a woman' will always be false. It is, however, the *statement*, as a description of possibilities, that in the first example is true. It does not tell us whether the actual prime minister is a man or a woman. The formal thinker will consider the possible as well as the actual and, indeed, will approach problems in this way.

In formal thought there is a reversal of the direction of thinking between *reality* and *possibility* in the subjects' method of approach. *Possibility* no longer appears merely as an extension of an empirical situation or of actions actually performed. Instead, it is *reality* that is now secondary to *possibility*. . . . Formal thinking is essentially hypothetico-deductive . . . deduction no longer refers directly to perceived realities but to hypothetical statements, i.e. it refers to propositions which are formulations of hypotheses, or which postulate facts or events independently of whether or not they actually occur. . . . Hence, conclusions are rigorously deduced from premises whose truth status is regarded only as hypothetical at first; only later are they empirically verified. This type of thinking proceeds *from* what is possible *to* what is empirically real. (Inhelder and Piaget, 1955, p. 251)

Therefore formal thinking leads to a different approach towards problem-solving. The child is now able to impose his or her own, logical, structure of hypothetical possibilities on the problem rather than accepting the structure of the problem that is given. When conducting an experiment concrete-level children will work with the materials before them in a trial-and-error fashion; they do not stand back and sort out what has to be done or enumerate the relevant variables. Formal thinkers will systematically generate all the possible hypotheses and manipulate one variable at a time while holding the others constant. Concrete thinkers take each proposition as it comes and do not make links between them. Their thinking is *interpropositional*, i.e. limited to a single proposition, whereas formal thinkers can consider the relationships *between* propositions, making their thought *intrapropositional*. The latter can deal with statements in the form 'If A . . . then B . . .' and realize the implications of 'If . . .' statements as well as the fact that the reverse, 'If B then A', is *not* entailed. The formal thinker is therefore able to perform operations on operations, or to think about the form of statements rather than just their content. While concrete operations are 'first degree' operations that apply to real objects and events, formal operations are 'second degree' operations that relate to statements made about the concrete operations and their real-life objects and events.

This notion of second degree operations also expresses the general characteristic of formal thought – it goes beyond the framework of transformations bearing directly on empirical reality (first degree operations) and subordinates it to a system of hypothetico-deductive operations, – i.e. operations which are possible. (Inhelder and Piaget, 1955, p. 254)

However, the stage of formal operations does not mean merely that the adolescent can perform more operations. The significant point is that they are combined into a new structure, as the child becomes aware of the *interdependence* of variables such as weight, time and speed, which had been considered in isolation at the concrete period. Once children have realized their interdependence they begin to unite them in various logical ways and it is this integrated structure of formal thought which makes it unique. Adolescent thought appears in the form of a lattice, or combinatorial system, because children have developed the ability to distinguish and order systematically all the possible combinations of a given number of elements. For example if they have four elements A, B, C and D, they can generate the sixteen possible combinations of them. In the same way the child can generate all the possible logical relations between two propositions each of which might be true or false.

The system of transformations known as the INRC group was thought to form a model for adolescent thought. In this, one of the operations has the properties of identity (I), which changes nothing, so that the identity operator maintains the status quo. The opposite of this is negation (N), in which everything is changed, so that all assertions become negations and all conjunctions (elements which are united) disjunctions, and vice versa. The reciprocal (R) transformation affects assertions and negations but leaves conjunctions and disjunctions unchanged. Finally the correlative (C) transformation affects conjunctions and disjunctions. By these means the child can understand the difference between (i) cancelling or undoing an effect (N in relation to I), as when a child will restore stolen money; and (ii) the compensation of this effect by another variable (R), for example when the child will work for the wronged person without pay until the equivalent amount of money is repaid, which can (iii) be cancelled by (C), when the person pays the child after all: C does not *eliminate* but *neutralizes* the effect. Piaget argued that in order to demonstrate the existence of a structure in this form the 'operational schemata' had to be studied, not just the operations which constitute them. He defines operational schemata as

> the concepts which the subject potentially can organise from the beginning of the formal level when faced with certain kinds of data, but which are not manifest outside these conditions . . . these operational schemata consist of concepts or special operations the need for which may be felt by the subject when he tries to solve certain problems. When the need is felt he manages to work them out spontaneously (or simply to understand – i.e. to rework them in cases when academic instruction has already dealt with the relevant concepts). Before the formal level he is not able to do this. (Inhelder and Piaget, 1955, p. 308)

Piaget studied several of these more specialized formal cognitive schemes; to illustrate them he gave several examples of formal thinking applied to problems. A child is shown four bottles containing colourless, odourless liquids, a small bottle with a dropper and an empty flask, and is asked to combine the liquids to make a yellow colour using all, or any, of the bottles as required. A formal solution requires the child to try all possible combinations, i.e. to make use of the sixteen possibilities minus the null class, rather than assuming that all the possibilities are exhausted if the liquid turns yellow after a trial-and-error mixing. The INRC group structure is exhibited in a task in which the child is shown a transparent U-shaped tube with liquid inside. On one side of the tube there is a piston. If weights are put on the piston it presses the water down on its side of the tube and, consequently, the water level rises in the other side of the tube. The child can vary the level by adding a weight to the piston so that X (the original water level) becomes X_1 (the new water level) (the operation of identity) or the child can cancel the operation by removing the weight (negation) so that X_1 returns to X. Alternatively the child can leave the weight alone but can substitute it by a heavier liquid so that X_1 becomes X by another means (a reciprocal operation). If the child then alters the density again, this time by using a lighter liquid, so that X becomes X_1, thus reversing the reciprocal by this new method: this is known as the correlate (C). The formal thinker realizes that given two variables there are two ways to produce an effect and two ways of counteracting it.

Piaget originally (Inhelder and Piaget, 1955) argued that the combinatorial operations and the INRC group were the structures which modelled formal thinking. In this he has been criticized for failing to make logical sense (Parsons, 1960), for failing to give an adequate account of formal operations (Lunzer, 1978), and for assuming that adolescent thought *is* best characterized as 'formal' (Neimark, 1975; Renner and Stafford, 1976; Kohlbert and Gilligan, 1971). Lunzer (1978) criticized Piaget's use of the INRC group as a 'unifying structure'. He noticed that concrete thinkers are particularly inclined to exhibit 'premature closure' to a problem – i.e. having found *a* solution, they are unwilling to accept that there may be others, or indeed that their own solution may be partial or contingent; whereas formal thinkers do accept lack of closure. To illustrate this he quotes a study by Matalon (1962) in which the child was shown a box with two compartments; there was a green light in one and a red light in the other. The child was told that 'whenever the red light is on the green light is on'. Not until the age of 11 or 12 did the children realize that if the red light was off they had no way of knowing whether the green was on or off; nor, if the green was on, could they tell what had happened to the red one. The younger children tended to say that if 'red on' means 'green on', then 'red off' means 'green off', and vice versa. In addition to acceptance of lack of closure older children will be able to use 'multiple interacting systems' so that they realize that one variable, for example area, may be conserved following a transformation when another, for example perimeter, will not be. Lunzer argued that to solve problems in this form required the use of multiple interacting systems but not the INRC group. Finally he did not believe that logical inference implied anything about thinking in general, regarding it only as a discrete aspect of thinking which could be facilitated or hindered by the content of the statements, so that likely, or concrete, premises are easier to argue correctly from than abstract or unlikely premises. In support of this it has been shown that people have difficulty when presented with Wason and Johnson-Laird's (1972) abstract four-card problem. In this problem the subject is presented with four cards and told the rule that 'If a card has a vowel on one side it has an even number on the other'. The subject has to 'name those cards and only those cards which need to be turned over in order to determine whether the rule is true or false'. However, if the content but not the structure of the task itself is modified (Johnson-

Laird *et al.*, 1972) so that the subject is shown envelopes and the rule is 'If a letter is sealed it has a five-penny stamp on it', subjects find the task much easier. In addition Wason and Shapiro (1971) found that four-card-problem performance was improved when the content was thematic, as when the rule was 'Every time I go to Manchester I go by car'. Thus content appeared to be highly influential.

There are, however, difficulties with the above argument. If subjects are familiar with the real-world content they will be aware of the nature of the relationship between two events and may therefore argue correctly, not because they understand the logic of the statement, but because they are familiar with the situation in reality. For example, if the experimenter says 'If the television is on then it is after 4 p.m.', it is not difficult for the subject to realize that if it is after 6 p.m. the television is not necessarily on, simply because such matters may form part of the subject's actual experience. Only a formal presentation of the problem can ensure that the person is approaching it as a formal problem and not relating it to personal experience. However, it may be that reflection on real-world experience of this kind leads the adolescent or adult to realize that 'if P then Q' does not imply 'if Q then P'.

The earlier work of Legrenzi (1971) suggests that people can be trained to solve problems formally, even when they have an abstract content, and that familiarity with the required logical system may be important. He taught his subjects all the possible classifications of relationship between antecedent and consequent and then tested them with Wason's four-card problem and found they were more likely to be correct than an untrained control group.

Another alternative view to Piaget's is one we have met before, which attributes the changes characteristic of adolescent thought to changes in task-specific component skills. Some writers use computer analogue models which stress people's 'operations' on 'knowledge states' and their increasing sophistication in selecting the appropriate operation (e.g. Case, 1978; Klahr and Siegler, 1978). Karplus (1981), although working within the Piagetian tradition, replaces the notion of 'stage' with that of 'reasoning patterns':

A reasoning pattern, such as seriation, conservation, or control of variables, is an identifiable and reproducible thought process directed at a type of task. . . . [reasoning patterns] do not refer to specific content, experiences or relationships . . . but . . . are concerned with certain recurring relationships. (p. 288)

He distinguishes between concrete and formal levels but says that the difference between his formulation and Piaget's is that 'we propose classifying the applications of a reasoning pattern rather than the developmental level of an individual' (p. 289). Thus, for example, classification applied at the concrete level would involve sorting objects on the basis of some perceived similarity, whereas at the formal level the similarity could be an abstract property. A teacher, if he or she looks at reasoning patterns in this way, can match the subject content to the child's reasoning pattern and realize that the same content may be approached using a concrete or a formal pattern. Karplus suggests that teachers should institute a 'learning cycle' consisting of three phases: 'explanation', 'concept induction' and 'concept application'. He illustrated this approach by the twelve-hour numerical relationships course to teach constant ratio, constant difference and constant sum problems, in which the exploratory phase involved the teacher presenting

two variable tables with the entries
$X = 4 \qquad 6$
$Y = 8 \qquad ?$
The students are challenged to propose values for the missing entries and to justify their suggestions with reference to illustrative examples. Many possibilities exist . . . $Y = 12$ (constant ratio), $Y = 10$ (constant difference) $Y = 6$ (constant sum). (p. 307)

Concept induction

presents the idea that numerical data by themselves are insufficient to determine the answer uniquely, and that other information – the situational context of the numerical data – must be taken into account to determine just which numerical relationship is most appropriate. (p. 307)

He then gives an example of an application exercise:

Two parachutists, Bill and Karen, are falling towards the ground with the same velocity. Bill jumped out of the plane later than Karen, so he is originally above her. Both Bill and Karen measure their altitude above ground. The two variables in this situation are — and —. The relationship between these variables is — because (please justify your answer) —. (p. 307)

One final criticism of Piaget is that his characterization of adolescent thought does not, in fact, model adolescent thought processes at all. Two forms of evidence are adduced in support of this. The first, often based on cross-cultural studies, maintains that formal reasoning of Piaget's type does not appear at all in some cultures (Dasen, 1977); and the second that even in cultures in which it does occur it is not the typical mode of thought, nor do people apply it to all the tasks for which it would be appropriate. A number of gloomy generalizations often accompany such studies. Flavell (1977) quotes two:

> Thus formal operational thinking, while emerging during adolescence, cannot be said to represent the characteristic mode of thought for that developmental period. (Martorano, 1974, p. 73; Flavell, 1977, p. 114)

> Logical reasoning, as reflected in consistent performance across a broad class of instances, does not appear until adolescence and even at that age is by no means a universal attainment of all adolescents. (Neimark, 1975, p. 570; Flavell, 1977, p. 115).

In support of this Renner and Stafford (1976) found that out of 588 American secondary-school pupils only 58 were formally operational, with 87 being transitional, 423 fully concrete and 20 early concrete. They then quote Kohlberg and Gilligan's (1971) comment that 'a large proportion of Americans never develop the capacity for abstract thought' and conclude:

> The curriculum in the secondary school has for years reflected what 'experts' thought should be there. The data in this research clearly demonstrate that such a procedure is not producing the best results. The time has come when the curriculum should be selected because it matches the intellectual needs of learners and not because of tradition or because some pressure group put it there. Schools are for children not for well-meaning but ill-informed adults. (p. 101)

Shayer (1980), having reviewed studies of the incidence of

formal thinking among adolescents, concluded that 'even in 1978 it is not possible to confirm or deny the validity of Piaget's account of formal operational thinking' (p. 711). The 1974 British survey (Shayer *et al.*, 1976; Shayer and Wylam, 1978), in which 11,200 children were tested, with nearly 2000 from each age group between 9 and 16 years, found that formal thinking was characteristic only of the top third of the pupils and that there was a very wide range of functioning in secondary education.

Karplus (1981) carried out a cross-cultural study of understanding of proportional reasoning to see whether education had any influence on the emergence of formal reasoning. Essentially, he asked the children how they could find the height of Mr Tall in small paperclips if they knew he was six large paperclips high and Mr Small was four, and they could measure Mr Small with small paperclips. He was able to divide the pupils' answers into four kinds: (1) intuitive, with no understanding of proportions; (2) additive, whereby only the initial absolute difference was taken into account; (3) transitional; and (4) ratio, when the children realized that Mr Tall's height was 1½ times Mr Small's and that this ratio had to be maintained across all changes in materials. Karplus's sample was 2000 early adolescents in three countries with at that time selective schooling – Austria, Germany and Great Britain – and three with comprehensive systems – Denmark, Sweden and Italy. The results showed that there were variations by country and by school organization (tables 2 and 3). He concluded that the ability to use proportional reasoning could be increased by reorganizing teaching. The low showing of the United States sample should be borne in mind when considering the views of researchers who claim that formal reasoning is not typical of the average adolescent. Karplus's findings indicate the need for more cross-cultural studies, since one cannot assume, for example, that what is the case in the United States is, necessarily, the case in Britain or Germany.

Piaget (1972a) considered at some length the problem of the absence of formal thinking in many adolescents' cognitive repertoire and suggested several hypotheses. The first was that all normal individuals can attain formal operations but only if the environment actualizes this potential. The second proposed that individual abilities become more differentiated with age, meaning that some people will not become formal thinkers.

Table 2 Response distributions on paper-clips task – form B in three countries with selective school systems (per cent)

Category	Austria (Vienna)[a]			Germany (Gottingen)[b]			Great Britain (London)[a]		
	(Top group)[c]	(Middle group)[d]	(Low group)[d]	(Top group)[c]	(Middle group)[c]	(Low group)[d]	(Top group)[c]	(Middle group)[c]	(Low group)[c]
Intuitive	5	6	8	4	1	25	2	9	19
Additive	6	26	52	2	17	25	3	11	44
Transitional	14	16	6	4	16	8	5	10	9
Ratio (number)	74 (298)	52 (189)	35 (104)	89 (92)	66 (119)	41 (107)	90 (87)	70 (117)	29 (172)
percent of age group	50	30	20	20	30	50	10	10	80
(average age)	(14.3)	(14.3)	(14.5)	(14.8)	(15.2)	(14.9)	(14.3)	(14.3)	(14.3)

Source: Karplus, 1981, p. 296.
Notes: [a] eighth grade.
[b] ninth grade (no eighth grades in session).
[c] segregated by sex.
[d] coeducational.
[e] coeducational or segregated by sex.

Table 3 Response distributions on paper-clips task – form B in three countries with comprehensive school systems (per cent)

Category	Italy (Rome)[a]			Denmark[b]	Sweden (Göteborg)[c]	
	(Upper middle)[f]	(Middle class)[f]	(Working class)[d]	(Middle class)[e]	(Middle class)[e]	(Working class)[d]
Intuitive	7	12	26	18	13	13
Additive	19	37	26	21	16	42
Transitional	5	8	18	25	16	20
Ratio	70	43	31	37	54	25
(number)	(161)	(110)	(196)	(397)	(98)	(179)
(average age)	(13.2)	(13.3)	(13.7)	(14.0)	(14.5)	(14.0)

Source: Karplus, 1981, p. 297.
Notes: [a]eighth grade.
[b]seventh grade (corresponding to eighth in US).
[c]seventh and eighth grades (corresponding to eighth and ninth in US).
[d]segregated by sex.
[e]coeducational.
[f]coeducational or segregated by sex.

Such a model of intellectual growth would be comparable to a fully expanded hand fan, the concentric layers of which would represent the successful stages of development whereas the sectors, opening wider towards the periphery, correspond to the growing differences in aptitude. (p. 205)

If this were the case 'our fourth period can no longer be characterised as a proper stage, but would already seem to be a structural advancement in the direction of specialisation' (p. 205). Piaget's third hypothesis combined aspects of the other two:

all normal subjects attain the stage of formal operations or structuring if not between 11–12 to 14–15 years in any case between 15 and 20 years. However, they reach this stage in different areas according to their aptitudes and their professional specialisations . . . the way in which these formal structures are used, however, is not necessarily the same in all cases. (p. 207)

Piaget saw all people as able to apply 'formal' thinking, i.e. thinking freed from its real-world content, but only to these areas in which they have specific understandings and expertise. His final view was:

It is one thing to dissociate the form from the content in a field which is of interest to the subject and within which he can apply his curiosity and initiative, and it is another to be able to generalise this same spontaneity of research and comprehension to a field foreign to the subject's career and interest. (p. 208)

While such a statement may well fit with the empirical evidence, what is not clear is *why* it should be so. If formal thinking enables the subject to dissociate form from content then it seems odd that content should determine when such a dissociation may take place. If, indeed, the subject really understands that 'if A then B' does not imply 'if B then A', he or she should be able to solve problems in this *form* even when totally ignorant of the properties of the content. Indeed one of the advantages of a 'formal' approach is that it frees the subject from having to know the characteristics of the contents to which the formal argument is applied. Thus subjects can decide on the truth or falsity of the proposition in the absence of factual knowledge. Similarly to translate emotive propositions into their logical forms can often make it easier to judge their truth or falsehood unclouded by their emotional overtones. A more likely hypothesis may be that the majority of people can think formally, and do think formally in certain contexts, but a minority think formally in the contexts Piaget chose as examples of formal thought. The majority could think formally in these contexts provided that doing so would not over-extend their available schemes.

While context may affect a person's ability to think formally, or at least to think in a more abstract or content-free manner, so too will this more advanced form of thinking affect the person's understanding of traditional school subjects. Piaget's experiments were largely in the field of mathematics or science and there have been some useful studies of the school science (Shayer, 1980) and mathematics curricula (Collis, 1976; Brown, 1979). These demonstrate both that formal operations are not achieved by all pupils and that formal thinking is a requirement of some aspects of the curriculum.

Shayer (1980) showed that Piagetian tests can predict a pupil's understanding of science, and the British Nuffield Ordinary-level chemistry syllabus was modified as a result. He argued that the syllabus of many science courses is suitable only for the operatory level of the top 20 per cent of the population and that the others achieve less than they could have done because of the mismatch between the course and their capabilities.

Collis (1976) related acceptance of lack of closure (ALC) and the ability to handle multiple interacting systems (MIS) to mathematical thinking. By the age of 7+ children will understand $2 + 2 = 4$ *but* the numbers have to be small and lead to a single outcome. By 10 they can use larger numbers and sequential closure, for example $2 + 2 + 2 = 6$. At 13, a formula can be used such that $A + B + C = D$ is meaningful but only if each letter has a one-to-one relationship with a number. Only at 16 will students consider relationships between variables rather than results of operations so that if $A + B + C = D$ they can consider the effect on D of doubling A and reducing B by a quarter without closure. Also, the young child can cope with simple relationships between variables but not with complex interactive relationships which require simultaneous variations. Only at the formal stage will young children realize that a single number can be arrived at by many possible operations on many possible numbers. Brown (1979) showed that when asked 'what can you say about "C" if C + D = 10 and C is less than D, 44% of second years, 41% of third years and 30% of fourth years gave only one number'. This may reflect the pupils' expectations due to the way mathematics, especially in the early years, is taught. They are often expected to look for one answer, and often one and only one is correct. They are less often asked to find different ways of arriving at answers although the use of micro-computers will enable them to write programs which will do just that. Brown held that, while Piaget's theory of concrete operations was useful for mathematics teaching, his formal theory was less useful in that solving problems in the form given above cannot be modelled by the INRC structure, although they do require operating on operations and are formal in that sense.

The need for formal thinking in other aspects of the school curriculum has also been assessed. Jurd (1978a, 1978b) considered the relevance of Piaget's ideas for history teaching. Although history is a more open system than science and necessarily less precise, she did find that 'the stages defined by logical operations and the strategies within these stages may be identified in history-type material' (Jurd, 1978b, p. 344). She tested pupils aged 11 to 18 by questioning them on three series of events which might have happened in three fictitious countries, Adza, Mulba and Nocha. The questions covered the pupils' understanding of vocabulary and their use of specific operating structures in order to test their understanding of, for example, causality, ordering or the balance of forces. For example, a question such as 'How could Henry have helped the landowners to buy imported goods?' required the pupils to conceptualize the balance of forces in history.

Jurd saw this as parallel to the U-shaped tube problem (see p. 124):

> Instead of the weight of the piston the weight of increased taxation was given, instead of the opposing density of the liquid the postulated desire of the landowners to buy imports was given, and instead of the concept of pressure the concept of a balance of resources and expenditure was given. (p. 331)

Her findings showed that the majority of pupils were operating at the concrete level, with a few sixth-formers showing a formal understanding of balance of forces. Finally the pupils' understanding of historical concepts was tested (questions XVI, XVII and XVIII in figure 2). Once again the difficulty of the questions did relate to the operatory level required for their solution so that the number, kind and relation of attributes within a concept made that concept more or less difficult to acquire. She concluded that 'From a knowledge of the sequence of development in logical operations, teachers may plan realistic sequences in understanding historical material' (p. 347).

Rhys (1972) studied children's ability to handle geography which is necessarily difficult for children below the formal level in requiring them to study men and women in unfamiliar environments and to interpret maps. His subjects were children aged 9 to 16. Five themes were chosen: soil erosion in an Andes Valley, Masai migration in East Africa, commercial grain-growing in Manitoba, intensive rice cultivation in Japan and crofter farming in the Outer Hebrides. The relevant information was given in prose passages, maps, photographs and statistical tables. He found four major response levels and, although there was fluctuation for individual children between levels, there was a qualitative sequence in response from the least to the most mature. The most mature took all the relevant variables into account and realized that their contribution had to be assessed in relation to each other. Since geography requires the child to appreciate the interaction between human beings and their environment he concluded that 'The achievement of equilibrium with respect to symbolic representation of unencountered "worlds" would seem to be critically dependent upon the emergence of a capacity for hypothetico-deductive reasoning' (Rhys, 1972, p. 260).

Cognition in adulthood and old age

To speak of cognitive 'development' in adult life and old age may be a misnomer. Flavell (1970) believed that the changes in adult life were much smaller than the universal and inevitable cognitive change characteristic of childhood and adolescence: 'my impression, then, is that the physiological changes that occur in normal adulthood do not lead to or support cognitive changes of the consistency, size, and kind that are mediated by the childhood growth process' (p. 249).

Nevertheless some studies do show increased performance at certain tasks during mature adult life. Adults show steady or slightly increased scores on the verbal sub-tests of intelligence

Figure 2 Some history-test items

XV Here are the same events for Adza and Mulba set out in columns and rows. Events in Nocha were very similar. List the events in Nocha (as given below) in the rows 1 to 5 under 'Nocha'.

Adza	Mulba
1 After his father's death Henry became king.	1 Having led his people to victory against invaders, Richard became dictator.
2 Henry wanted to increase the number of large cargo ships, so that more goods would be imported.	2 Once he had power Richard desired more land and wealth.
3 Landowners' taxes were increased to pay for cargo ships.	3 All men between 18 and 25 years of age had to go into military service.
4 Landowners had little money to improve their farms.	4 Few young men were left in factories and on farms.
5 Farms produced less and landowners had no money to buy imported goods.	5 Production fell, goods could not be exported to nearby countries and living conditions became worse.
6 Landowners refused to pay any more taxes.	6 There was a successful plot to kill Richard.
7 The king agreed to have an advisory council of representative landowners.	7 The people elected a group of other leaders.

tests, which assess verbal fluency, vocabulary, verbal reasoning, etc. There is no decline until after age 60, if then (Doppelt and Wallace, 1955). Denney and Palmer (1980) showed that performance on tasks relating to practical problems increased over the years until approximately age 50. However, increases in performance and age of peak performance may depend on the subject area chosen for research. Lehman (1953, 1954, 1958, 1962, 1965, 1966) found that, in general, people were professionally at their most productive during their thirties but that this peak was earlier, in the late twenties and early thirties, for mathematicians and chem-

Events in Nocha (to be listed in correct order down the column)

A   Most money from taxes was spent on defence.
B   The leaders wanted to build up the army so Nocha would be safe.
C   Three military leaders were elected to rule Nocha together.
D   Standards of education declined and there were no more cultural festivals, which the people had enjoyed.
E   Less money was available for education, music and drama.

	Nocha	Similarities
1		
2		
3		
4		
5		
6		
7		

XVI   Considering what happened in Adza and Mulba, fill in what might have happened next in Nocha (rows 6 and 7).
XVII   In the column headed 'Similarities', say in what way the events listed in each country (across rows) are similar (leave out row 5).
XVIII Events in all three countries showed a change towards ....

Source: Jurd, 1978b, pp. 322–33

ists and later, between 45 and 55, for those employed in the humanities and for astronomers. Similar results, showing a peak between 30 and 40, were found for workers in creative areas, in practical invention and for chess-players. These figures were supported by Manniche and Falk (1957) who showed that the work for which scientists subsequently gained Nobel prizes was usually carried out around the age of 30. However, research on industrial performance does not reveal a decrease after the mid-forties except in tasks which require speed of work (Arvey and Mussio, 1973; De La Marre and Shephard, 1958). Denney (1982) suggests that experience or 'exercise' may be a significant factor determining whether an ability increases, remains static or declines from the level attained in late adolescence and early adulthood. She distinguished 'unexercised ability' from 'optimally exercised' ability. The former

> reflects what a normal healthy individual would be able to do if that individual were not given any training or exercise in the particular ability in question. . . . [it] is proposed to be a function of *both* biological potential and normal, standard, environmental experience. (pp. 818–19)

The latter

> reflects the maximum biological potential given a normal environment and optimal exercise and/or training of the ability in question. (p. 819)

While both forms of ability decline with age, performance on unexercised abilities seems much weaker because of the lower level attained originally.

Many studies point either to a general linear decline in abilities or to a more sudden decline in later life, with old age seen as a period of decreasing cognitive power. When cross-sectional studies of Piagetian tasks were carried out, old people were found to perform more like young children on classificatory tasks (Cicirelli, 1976; Denney, 1974a, 1974b), to be more animistic (Dennis and Mallinger, 1949), more egocentric (Rubin, 1974) and to be less likely to display formal thought than young adults (Clayton and Overton, 1976; Kuhn *et al.*, 1977). However, findings on performance on conservation tasks were mixed. Sanders *et al.* (1966) found considerable age differences in the ability to give spatial conserving responses plus justifications. In their study 84 per cent of the youngest group, aged 20 to 39, were correct, as were 72.1 per cent of the middle group, aged 45 to 59, but the figure dropped to 22.6 per cent of the oldest group whose average age was 72 years. In support of this, Papalia (1972) found that 100 per cent of young subjects understood conservation of substance but only 62 per cent of the elderly. Rubin (1976) demonstrated the same perfect understanding among the young, dropping to 50 per cent of the elderly for conservation of weight. However, Papalia (1972) found no differences in conservation of number, and Selzer and Denney (1980) found similar performances in tests of conservation of substance, weight and volume between elderly and middle-aged subjects. It is possible that conservation ability is lost in the reverse order in which it was developed so that volume, which develops last, would decay first, and Denney (1982) suggests that use of an ability may halt its decline, and so the forms of conservation which are used in daily life do not decline.

It has been proposed (Hooper *et al.*, 1971) that cognitive decline in old age reflects the cognitive development of childhood, but in reverse, even to the extent that there may be 'a sequential order of regression which would involve the formal period tasks first and the concrete operational skills at a still later point' (p. 15). It does seem that formal thinking declines, but other results go further and indicate that cognition in old age mirrors cognition in early childhood in that both are less differentiated than in older childhood and younger adult life. Thus a general factor of intelligence is thought to be more salient and there are less discrete, uncorrelated and specific factors reflecting various cognitive abilities (Green and Berkowitz, 1964).

Tests of problem-solving ability also indicated that older people perform less well than younger ones, especially if the material is abstract and removed from real life (Arenberg, 1974). However, Denney and Palmer (1980) found a decline with both real-life and experimental tasks in old age. On a twenty-question task old people were shown (Denney and Wright, 1978) to behave at a less complex level than younger adults and not to ask abstract general-ized questions such as 'Can you wear it?' but, like young children, to ask closed particular questions such as 'Is it my hat?' Denney *et al.* (1979) also found that both children and elderly adults responded similarly to training. Most mental operations are done more slowly with age; the old possibly process at a different rate to the young; and old people are less flexible in problem-solving. Indeed Salthouse (1982) argued that 'increased age effect in adulthood seems to be a disadvantage in most laboratory tests of cognitive processes' (p. 201). However, Charness's work with chess-players (1981a, 1981b, 1981c) indicates that experience could compensate for age.

There has been a considerable amount of work on memory changes in adulthood and, especially, old age. There seem to be both qualitative and quantitative changes at all stages of the memory cycle. Although the precise problem has not been identified, at the encoding stage the elderly seem to have particular problems possibly because they have difficulty translating visual information with cognitive representations. They also use less efficient strategies by not using mediators to aid memory or, like young children (see p. 97), organization. Heron and Craik (1964) found no differences between the younger and older adults when they asked them to remember material which could not be organized, but a difference in favour of the young when it could. With storage in general there seems little difference over short periods but the older subjects were worse when the interval was longer than twenty-four hours (Salthouse, 1982). The studies of retrieval have had mixed results, but once again familiarity and use seem significant. Murrell and Humphries (1978) compared the performances of young adults, with an average age of 25 years, and of older adults, with an average age of 57 years, on a speech-shadowing task. Both groups contained some subjects who were experienced simultaneous translators and some who were not. The percentages of errors made were as follows: experienced older adults 22 per cent, inexperienced older adults 59 per cent, experienced younger adults 23 per cent and inexperienced younger adults 35 per cent.

It is possible that there are age differences in the functioning of metamemory. The elderly use less efficient strategies but whether this is due to an inability to use them or a failure to know of them is less clear. It does seem odd that the understanding that one *can* use strategies should be lost whereas a failure to do what one once could do is a characteristic of ageing in general. Indeed Perlmutter (1978) found no differences between young, middle-aged, and elderly adults in knowledge about memory, and that adults of all ages were able to make equally realistic predictions of their ability to recall information. It is possible that older adults suffer no deterioration in metamemory, and therefore know what they should do, but do have difficulty carrying out memory tasks.

While older people seem, in the laboratory, to remember less well than younger ones there may be a selective aspect to this.

Labouvie-Vief and Schell (1982) argue on the basis of evidence from many experiments that

> whether assessed by more global measures of recall accuracy or more analytic measures of retrieval speeds, older adults do not appear to suffer from a generalised central deficit. Indeed it appears that their processing efficiency is lawfully related to their familiarity with task materials, just as it is for the young. (p. 839)

They further maintain that the behaviour of older people may be adaptive to the demands of life at their stage and hence no different from the adaptations made by younger people.

> a loss of flexibility, increased specialization and an increasing integration of the mnemonic system with ecological demands are a regular concomitant of developmental progression. Therefore many of the changes observed in ageing adults are not, in principle, different from those observed at other developmental periods. (p. 842)

There are several methodological problems relating to studies of cognition and ageing. The most obvious source of error is the contamination of age differences with cohort differences which can occur in cross-sectional studies. Thus, if a cross-sectional study in 1980 studied formal thinking in a group of 20-year-olds, 40-year-olds and 60-year-olds plus, one cannot tell whether differences between the groups truly represent *age* effects or the fact that the 20-year-olds were born in 1960, the 40-year-olds in 1940, and the 60+ group before 1920. Nor can we tell whether the 60+ group was like the 20-year-olds when they were themselves 20. All we can tell is that in 1980 people aged 60+ show less ability to think formally than those of 20. Thus we can show *differences* in performance between people of different ages but are not necessarily able to say that these differences are due to their different ages. We have seen that formal thinking may be affected by schooling, and since the schooling of the majority of older people was much more limited than is the schooling of young people today some of the differences in cognition may reflect this historical fact.

While longitudinal studies in which the *same* people are tested at different ages may seem to avoid this source of error, they can have problems of their own in that if the subjects are tested every few years an external event may cause a change in performance which would be incorrectly attributed to an age change; also people drop out, and this is not random, for it is the more able who tend to remain. However, the few longitudinal studies that have been undertaken suggest that while a decline is still apparent with age it appears later than the cross-sectional studies imply (e.g. Arenberg, 1974). Denney (1982) summarizes the findings of the two forms of study and their problems as follows:

> most of the cognitive abilities exhibit age differences that are reflective of age changes. . . . Cross-sectional studies suggest that the decline begins at an earlier age and is more extensive than longitudinal studies indicate. It is not clear whether the quantitative discrepancies in the cross-sectional and longitudinal studies are a result of the cross-sectional studies overestimating age changes because age change is confounded with cohort differences or whether the longitudinal studies underestimate age change because of the problems associated with selective survival. (p. 811)

A further problem is to distinguish between the effects of ageing *per se* on cognition and the effects of the physical and mental diseases which often accompany old age and which would, themselves, affect cognition irrespective of the age of the person. Thus Chance *et al.* (1978) found that differences in performance in conservation tasks disappeared when the subjects were matched for health and education. An interesting finding from several longitudinal studies is that there are changes in test scores as death approaches, and indeed that changes in performance, in the absence of illness, may signal the onset of death (Siegler, 1975). A longitudinal study of twins which began in 1940 (Blum *et al.*, 1973) found that a twin showing a reduced performance on certain sub-tests, called 'critical loss', when in his or her sixties and seventies was significantly more likely to die within five years than was a twin who showed no such reduced performance. (This raises the question of whether death is a slow process affecting the whole person, with the final illness being merely a *coup de grâce* to a weakened organism rather than the sole cause of death.)

Salthouse (1982) suggests that abilities which remain stable or improve with age are difficult to study in the laboratory, as are 'normal' activities, due to the difficulty of specifying exactly what they require. He also points to the fact that researchers do not publish negative findings and therefore studies which find no age effects do not appear in the journals, possibly giving a false impression of decay with age.

While considerable individual differences are found in these studies, and severe methodological problems in general, there seems little evidence of widespread overall decrease in cognitive ability before the age of 65 to 70. Indeed, the evidence indicates generally an increase up to 50, certainly in abilities which are used. There is probably, however, a steady decline in abstract problem-solving from early adulthood. This indicates that adults, at least up to age 50 and probably up to 65, are likely to be able to retrain successfully, especially if the new specialty has cognitive characteristics which are similar to their current expertise. These findings also suggest that adults would benefit from the opportunity of practising skills which they are not required to use in their daily work, for after the age of 25, so far as cognitive abilities are concerned, the moral appears to be 'use it or lose it'.

Individual differences

Once cognitive development reaches the formal stage, considerable differentiation in functioning can be found between individuals, especially with reference to the subject areas within which they perform most competently. By the end of their secondary schooling most pupils will know which subjects they prefer and feel most competent in. The more academically inclined of them will also have chosen an area of study to pursue in further or higher education, a decision which may affect most of their adult working life. It is possible that subject choice reflects social and cultural factors as much as cognitive competence, although greater skill in verbal, numerical or spatial ability may lead an adolescent to concentrate on one group of subjects rather than another. In addition psychometric measures of 'intelligence' or 'creativity' have also been found to correlate with subject choice, but such measures go beyond cognition as such.

It appears that there are sex differences in subject choice but that these are of much greater magnitude than could be accounted for by the hypothesized sex differences in cognition. Maccoby

143

(1966) maintained that there did appear to be some differences in intellectual performance between the sexes. In a later work (Maccoby and Jacklin, 1974), she said:

> The earlier argument began by assuming the existence of certain sex differences in intellectual performance that have not turned out to be consistently present; it then attempted to explain these on the basis of personality differences that have also proved to be more myth than reality. In view of this, the senior author can do little more than beg the reader's indulgence for previous sins. (p. 133)

In their more recent work they reviewed the literature on sex differences on perception, learning and memory and concluded that

> beginning in early infancy, the two sexes show a remarkable degree of similarity in the basic intellectual processes of perception, learning and memory. (p. 61)

In general, it seems that the evidence for sex differences in cognition is really rather slim. Archer and Lloyd (1982) reviewed the evidence for sex differences in spatial and verbal abilities. It has been found that males excel in tasks requiring them mentally to rotate figures such as piles of blocks so as to imagine them in a different orientation, and at finding a simpler shape hidden in a complex pattern as assessed by the embedded figures test (EFT) (Witkin *et al.*, 1962). It appears that these skills could facilitate male performance in geometry or chess but not in other branches of mathematics or in the natural sciences. The evidence for women's greater verbal fluency (Maccoby and Jacklin, 1974) was not confirmed by Brimer's (1969) study of 8000 English school children's listening skills, and Fairweather (1976) showed males to score slightly higher than females. Lloyd and Archer concluded:

> The evidence for a female superiority in verbal abilities is not as convincing as that which has been martialled to show a male advantage in spatial skills. The picture which emerges from the examination of careful tests of intellectual functioning is one of limited differences between men and women. (p. 37)

Similarly Sherman (1978) argued that, while females do appear to show greater verbal proficiency at the infant and pre-school stage, reported adult differences seem to be small. Her conclusion concerning male superiority in spatial ability and mathematics was:

> There now seems to be general agreement that no difference between the sexes in favour of males is observable until adolescence. . . . A similar situation may well exist in mathematics. . . . The Wisconsin Study found no differences until age fifteen . . . the sexes overlap tremendously and sex has accounted for, at most, a few percent of the variance. (pp. 65–6)

These small sex differences in cognitive ability cannot explain the wide divergence in subject choice illustrated by Murphy's (1980) table, reproduced in Archer and Lloyd (1982) and here (see table 4).

The psychometric measures are intended to be measures of ability rather than attainment, although it is in fact difficult to separate the two. It may well be that subject choice reflects attainment of skills rather than ability in certain cognitive areas. Shayer and Wylam (1978) did find some sex differences in science performance, and Shayer (1980) commented:

Table 4 Candidates in 13 Advanced-level subjects (summer 1977)

Subject	Male entries (thousands)	Percentage of total	Female entries (thousands)	Percentage of total
Art	10.92	41.9	15.17	58.1
Biology	18.40	49.4	18.84	50.6
British Constitution	11.89	64.6	6.51	35.4
Chemistry	27.48	70.6	11.47	29.4
Economics	28.57	72.9	10.60	27.1
English	22.56	33.5	44.74	66.5
French	8.09	32.1	17.09	67.9
General studies	15.95	57.3	11.89	42.7
Geography	23.26	64.7	12.67	35.3
History	19.25	49.1	19.92	50.6
Physics	37.07	82.2	8.02	17.8
Pure and applied maths	37.01	77.4	10.78	22.6
Sociology	5.04	31.9	10.76	68.1

Source: Archer and Lloyd, 1982, p. 192 (from Murphy, 1980).

The large scale survey . . . found some sex differentials. Anyone who has tried to teach physics to 12/13 year old girls will have encountered an obvious one: the experiments, and the way they are handled intellectually are of very low appeal. Equally, girls do like live animals, and anything to do with the animals' young. This difference between boys and girls is obviously related to their different future roles in adult life, yet it reaches back to be a major factor in motivation for people in early adolescence . . . in looking for a new content for secondary science work . . . one must consider what experiences are most suitable for the realisation of science processes for both boys and girls in the key periods 11–13, 13–15 and in late adolescence. (p. 725)

This comment is interesting in that it raises the whole problem of whether curriculum planners should work with the current stereotypes, and hence reinforce stereotypical gender differences, or attempt to oppose them. The latter may result in more girls developing their potential for science and engineering or may merely drive girls away as, Shayer suggests, is happening now. It may well be that scientific concepts need to be illustrated by specific contents chosen in such a way as to appeal to groups of adolescents who have previously found the content uninteresting and hence have not developed an understanding of the underlying concept. At this age many pupils will judge knowledge as worthwhile only in so far as it is seen to be of immediate use. They have a concrete approach rather than a formal perspective. This needs to be borne in mind when selecting curriculum contents.

There has been some attempt to link individual differences in choice of subject or general cognitive performance to differences in what is known as 'cognitive style', or the way in which people construct their view of reality. Kelly (1955) argued that individuals may structure, or represent, their environments in a more or less complex way. He measured this by the role construct repertory test (Rep. Test) and this has been used to assess people's 'cognitive complexity'. Vacc and Vacc (1973) modified this test for use with children. While adults show individual variability on this measure, children are thought to show a developmental progression, with greater integration of constructs appearing with age (Bannister and Mair, 1968). In support of this, Rushton and Wiener (1975) found that 11-year-olds gained significantly higher cognitive complexity scores than 7-year-olds. Harvey *et al.* (1961)

made a further distinction related to the way people process information. They argued that sensory input is processed by 'differentiation', i.e. distinguishing between stimuli on various simple or more complex dimensions, and 'integration', i.e. the use of cognitive rules to consider the dimensions used in relationship to one another. Thus a person low in differentiation might categorize another person by age and sex, whereas a more complex differentiator would use more categories. Having differentiated the various dimensions by which to categorize the person or object, the thinker must integrate them in simple or more complex ways, by giving them equal or variable weightings, etc. In other words the more complex a person's thinking the more aspects of a situation he or she is able to take into account.

Probably the best-known approach to cognitive style is that of Witkin *et al.* (1962). They divided people into those who were, cognitively, predominantly 'field dependent' and those who were 'field independent', and related this categorization to personality measures. 'Field independence' means that a person's perceptions of an object are independent of the surrounding environment, so that he or she can more easily distinguish figure from ground or discern a simple figure in a complex pattern. The more global view of the 'field dependent' individual means that he or she is less able to distinguish in that way, and dependence on the surrounding environment leads to a more holistic mode of perception. Thus the person who is most able to differentiate would be the one who is also most likely to be field-independent. Witkin and Goodenough (1981) argue that field-independent individuals are better able to restructure their perceptions and cognitions and hence have greater flexibility in thinking and problem-solving. They believe that, on the evidence to date, while the ability to restructure may be limited to the spatio-visual material, on the other hand it may be a more general cognitive ability, with extensions to verbal and auditory tasks. Powers and Lis (1977) showed that children with higher embedded figures test (EFT) scores scored higher than did low EFT-scorers on linguistic tasks requiring active/passive grammatical transformations. If the child was given statements in the active or passive and then questioned on these in either the active or the passive, low EFT-scorers could cope with active/active or passive/passive combinations, whereas high EFT-scorers could cope with both. Witkin and Goodenough (1981) discuss whether field independence–dependence is a 'style' or an 'ability' and argue that it should be conceived of as a 'style' or way of thinking.

> In our current conception the most general dimension of cognitive functioning that has been identified is a dimension of individual differences in the extent of autonomy of external referents. In several ways this dimension may be seen to conform with the concept of style (manner of moving toward a goal) rather than the concept of ability (competence in goal attainment). . . . The model we have outlined views the development of field dependence–independence as multilinear. It proposes that the greater openness of field-dependent people to external sources of information is likely to stimulate the development of interpersonal competences, but does not encourage the development of cognitive restructuring skills. (pp. 58, 60)

For field independence the reverse is true:

> the primary developmental investments of field-dependent and field-independent people are seen as being made in different domains. (p. 61)

This analysis accords with the view argued here that late adolescents and adults, while all are able to think formally, may use this ability in different contexts and may have a preferred mode of thinking, namely the mode most appropriate for the context in which they are most interested. The culmination of cognitive development is therefore the attainment of a stage in which individuals are able to use their powers of thought to further their personal interests and concerns. While initially able to think in other ways people may not choose to do so and this choice may mean that while some cognitive approaches atrophy through disuse others will increase in power as a reflection of adult competencies.

7

Conclusion

This book has presented an account of cognitive development from birth through maturity to old age. Each chapter discussed a major stage in the individual's development. The fact that four-fifths of this book has been devoted to the years from birth to 12, leaving only one-fifth for the rest of the life span, is an indication of the disproportionate amount of research into cognitive development in childhood and youth, resulting in the virtual neglect of maturity and old age. It is true that development is more rapid and more apparent during the early years but this does not mean that development stops with early adolescence.

The first chapter considered infancy during which the foundations for later growth are laid. This should not be taken to imply that experiences in infancy determine future development, but its influence is pervasive. The human infant is born with a wide range of evolutionary adaptations which enable him or her to pay selective attention to those aspects of the environment which are most necessary for survival, both physical and psychological, as a member of the human species. Infants have been found to have an organized system for visual perception which forms the basis for subsequent development but which also has some features which require experience in order to develop fully. Infants' acute auditory system may be selectively attuned to human language. However, these are skills which the human infant possibly shares with non-human primates, lending weight to Scarr-Salapatek's argument that infant intelligence evolved before we separated from the non-human primates and hence is different in kind from later, symbolically mediated intelligence. During this period infant cognition moves from a stage when the infant does not distinguish itself from its surroundings, nor the discrete aspects of these surroundings, to, at about 2 years, being able to differentiate many aspects of the environment, to understand some of the properties of objects, and to form internal 'concepts' of these objects thus enabling the infant to think about an object or an event in its absence.

Piaget argued that the origins of intelligence lay in action, i.e. he saw the infant as, essentially, acting upon the environment in response to environmental stimulation. However, his theory seems to ignore the social aspect of the infant's world. An approach to infant intelligence which has grown in importance over the last decade is one which stresses the innate sociability of the human infant and the significance of this social orientation for cognitive development. Infants respond differently to physical objects and to people, seeking to communicate with the latter but to manipulate or explore the physical qualities of the former.

Trevarthen argues that infants are primarily motivated to co-operate with other humans and that it is this motive which has the strongest influence on cognition. Interestingly this view exactly parallels a change of emphasis in theories of personality development. Freud had argued that the infant's prime motivation is to reduce instinctual tension, but the later 'object relations' school, associated with the work of Fairbairn, Winnicott and Guntripp, maintained that, on the contrary, the infant's main aim is to seek personal relationships and it is this desire to 'be in relationship' with another human being which motivates many of its early actions. It appears that two different approaches to infant behaviour have come to a similar conclusion regarding the significance of the social in infant development. Language and pre-linguistic communication have a crucial role to play in the origins of interpersonal exchange. It has been argued that the process of early language development is the same for all human infants although, obviously, the language they learn may be very different. The impetus to learn language may be the infant's wish to communicate meaning. In this view the intention to communicate precedes the understanding of how to do so.

This early, adaptive, socially motivated form of intelligence, because of its evolutionary history, has less individual variability than later forms of intelligence. All non-handicapped children can be expected to show the forms of behaviour characteristic of this stage and to attain all forms of sensori-motor intelligence given minimal environmental stimulation. Indeed, suppressing these early forms of behaviour is very difficult indeed. The extent to which infants will use and develop these early skills does depend on their environments – for example, while all infants will try to communicate with other humans their subsequent skill in so doing will depend, at least in part, on the success of their early efforts. Attempts to study environmental variables and their influence on infant behaviour have led to the conclusion that one cannot speak, generally, about 'good' or 'bad' environments. Rather, some environments are better for one form of development, others for another. What the infant needs is a range of experiences and forms of stimulation from significant figures in the environment.

There have been some attempts to educate parents to provide the kind of stimulation required for satisfactory infant development, but such programmes cannot operate in isolation from the social context of living. In order for parents to be able to foster their children's cognitive growth it is essential that they feel themselves supported and have at least the minimal requirements with respect to housing and income. If these basic requirements are not met then it is possible, indeed probable, that these parents will be unable to operate effectively and the cycle of deprivation will continue.

In the 3 years between the end of infancy and the start of compulsory schooling, which are discussed in chapter 2, the child will be in the midst of the stage called 'pre-operational' by Piaget. It should not be seen as a period in which the child fails to do what older children and adults can do but one in which she (or he) is trying to make sense of the world given the knowledge she has. This will often mean that her conception of reality will differ from

151

the one she will, necessarily, come to in time but this later understanding can only develop out of these earlier attempts. It is only by trying, reassessing, and trying again that adult forms of thought will develop once the more mature strategy is seen by the child as being more appropriate for solving the problem before her. Pre-operational thinking represents the best form of cognitive adaptation that the child can devise at that time. It is therefore truly a stage on the way to mature thinking and not a wrong turning which needs to be corrected before the child can continue on the right path. Having said this, it is still the case that the thinking of these young children is characterized by concentrating on one aspect of a situation to the exclusion of others. This is particularly apparent in children's tendency to be fixated on their own point of view. They also cannot consider, easily, reversing an action. On the other hand they are developing notions of qualitative identity by realizing that an object, despite apparent changes in colour, size, etc., will be qualitatively the 'same' object. There is also considerable development in this period of the 'semiotic functions', or in the child's ability to represent to herself the outside world and her own actions and experiences. This ability to represent knowledge in memory is the heart of cognition. By the age of 5 language development is almost completed. The simple utterances of the 2-year-old are by then transformed into sentences which are similar, syntactically, to those of adults and by means of which the child can convey a wide range of meanings. Inevitably, children will have a more limited vocabulary than will adults and some children will be more articulate than others, i.e. have greater communicative competence, but for almost all non-handicapped children linguistic competence is fully developed by the time they start school. In the pre-school period it is possible to start investigating the development of memory, particularly the development of metamemory which enables the child to think about memory as a process which she can improve by employing relevant strategies, such as rehearsal.

It is possible that at this time environmental influences are beginning to affect, not the child's cognition as such, but the way in which she will respond to cognitive demands. Even at this early age some children are able to think about their own thinking to the extent of realizing that they will be able to learn in the future something that they do not know in the present, whereas other children are not able to separate themselves from their thinking in this way. A 'problem solving' environment which encourages autonomy and self-help in the child may facilitate this form of cognitive decentering.

Chapter 3 considered the early school years of 5 to 8 in which children first meet the demands of formal schooling. These are important transitional years which will, in Piaget's view, see the start of 'operational' thinking or the internalization of the earlier overt actions together with greater sophistication in the use of symbols. Most children will begin to classify correctly, to seriate, to develop a concept of number and to conserve. Schooling requires both that the child develops these concepts and masters the complex task of decoding the printed word. The child's memory will develop more fully at this age, in particular the ability to order objects to be remembered into categories as an aid to memory, a feat which would have been impossible before she had learnt to categorize in general. At school social interaction can facilitate cognitive development since this is the first time that the child has been intentionally taught as a member of a social group. Cognition will advance if a child compares her responses with those of another and then restructures her own. Merely exposing the child to a more mature cognitive model does not seem to facilitate cognitive change in the same way.

School requires the child to have some understanding of what 'learning' means together with an awareness of the appropriate strategies to use when asked to 'learn' something. The development of this form of metacognition is a gradual process, much of which takes place during the middle school years of 8 to 12, discussed in chapter 4. At this stage children's thinking while 'operational' is also 'concrete'. In using the term 'concrete operational' to describe this form of thinking Piaget meant to draw attention to its *structure* and its limitations in being confined to a present reality and unable to comprehend the possible or the abstract. Piaget believed that when faced with a problem the child's characteristic method of approach and attempts at solution could best be explained by positing the existence of 'operations', or internalized actions which were combined to form 'structures', the form of which could best be modelled by the nine 'groupements'. During these years schooling itself may facilitate the development of cognitive processes but there is a powerful argument which says that this is only so in non-literate cultures. In cultures which are, generally, literate the influence of school on the process of cognition may be minimal. This does not mean that schooling may not be influential in other ways, especially in developing metacognition which is increasingly seen to be implicated in many forms of learning.

Chapter 5 considered adolescent thinking when 'formal thinking', or the ability to use abstractions and systematically consider possibilities, develops. Formal thinking may not be developed by all the people in a culture nor be the characteristic mode of thinking of most people. But what is characteristic of adolescents and adults is that it is possible for them, in certain circumstances and with reference to certain contents, to think formally. Formal thinking implies a different orientation towards problem-solving. The formal thinker will begin by considering what could be causing the problem or how the solution could be arrived at. She or he would then check all her or his various hypotheses in a systematic manner. The non-formal thinker will seek a single solution and, having arrived at one which seems satisfactory, will go no further. Adolescent thought has also been described as the application of different forms of reasoning patterns to problems. The importance of understanding the nature of adolescent thought when teaching adolescents cannot be overstressed. There is nothing to be gained by expecting pupils to solve problems which require the utilization of schemes of thought which they have not developed. However, the presentation of such problems when the pupils are on the edge of formal thinking may facilitate its emergence.

During adult life cognitive development in general slows down although performance will continue to increase up to about the age of 50, in particular in those areas of thought in which there has been continued practice. In contrast, a faster decline will be apparent when a cognitive process or ability is not used. The question of cognitive decline in older age is controversial. Obtaining representative samples of the aged poses many problems as does the difficulty of distinguishing the effects of age, as such, from the effects of illness and disease which can accompany old age. It seems that, generally, no decline in cognitive processes is apparent until well after the age of retirement. However, extreme old age is associated with a decline in some abilities, especially memory and abstract problem solving. The homogeneity of cognition in infancy is balanced by the wide range of individual differences apparent in adults in terms of levels of ability in general, cognitive style, subject choice and specific areas of expertise. Nevertheless, the cognitive *processes* of adults are similar in that all can perceive stimuli, represent knowledge in memory and retrieve such knowledge when they wish to use it in their daily lives. The differences reflect the use to which these powers are put by adults. Infants, necessarily, have less choice as to how they use their cognitive abilities.

The direct application of theories of cognitive development to educational practice is not yet possible although educators may benefit from being aware of the contents of such theories. There are two dangers in attempting to make direct applications. First, the theory may be oversimplified as has happened when Piagetian theory is reduced to a description of 'stages' and, secondly, there may be a desire to apply parts of the theory without taking account of the theory as a whole as when learning in 'groups' is advocated without realizing that the composition of such groups may be crucial. Both of these attempts at application trivialize and distort, reducing psychology to little more than a justification for current educational practice. If cognitive development can be modelled by a spiral then similarity in process and diversity of outcome at different ages is to be expected. A possible implication for education is that any group of children of any age can be seen as being, above all, alike in sharing the same basic cognitive processes. Just as they can all breathe or digest so they can all perceive, remember, use symbols, reason and problem solve. However, each child is also unique and therefore children will use these powers differently depending on their previous knowledge and experience, present context and the present task. Diversity of performance reflects the children's individual use of cognition not their cognitive competence in general. Since all humans have the same underlying cognitive abilities simply because they are human, it is sterile to attempt to classify people in general and for all time on the basis of specific performances on certain dates. Educators may wish to assist individuals to assess for themselves how they are using their cognitive processes at any one time so as to plan what their next move should be. By these means learners can become involved in the process of their own learning.

When a child fails simply drawing her (or his) attention to the failure of performance is unlikely to improve that performance. No doubt the child already knows she cannot read, or spell, or multiply. Her performance is more likely to benefit by showing her that just as she can control her breathing by panting, breathing deeply or holding her breath, so too she can control her thinking. The child needs to understand that there are specific strategies for specific tasks and that the generation and use of these strategies is something she can do for herself.

To study 'cognition' is to study that which is similar in all humans. To study 'development' is to concentrate on that which is dissimilar. Education may be seen as a process which, beginning from what we have in common, assists individuals to create their own particularity by their own agency.

Suggestions for further reading

Chapter 2

Beller, E.K. (1979) 'Early intervention programmes', in Osofsky, J.D. (ed.) *Handbook of Infant Development*, New York, Wiley, 852–94.

Bower, T.G.R. (1982) *Development in Infancy*, 2nd edn, San Francisco, Freeman.

Cohen, L.B. and Salapatek, P. (eds) *Infant Perception: From Sensation to Cognition*, vol. 1: *Basic Visual Processes*, vol. 2: *Perception of Space, Speech and Sound*, New York, Academic Press.

Lewis, M. (ed.) (1976) *Origins of Intelligence*, New York, Plenum.

Oates, J. (1979) *Early Cognitive Development*, London, Croom Helm.

Piaget, J. and Inhelder, B. (1969) *The Psychology of the Child*, London, Routledge & Kegan Paul (originally published, 1966).

Chapter 3

Baddeley, A.D. (1976) *The Psychology of Memory*, New York, Basic Books.

Boden, M.A. (1979) *Piaget*, London, Fontana.

Dale, P.S. (1976) *Language Development*, 2nd edn, New York, Holt, Rinehart & Winston.

de Villiers, P.A. and de Villiers, J.G. (1979) *Early Language*, London, Fontana.

Ferguson, C.A. and Slobin, D.I. (eds) (1973) *Studies of Child Language Development*, New York, Holt, Rinehart & Winston.

Flavell, J.H. (1977) *Cognitive Development*, Englewood Cliffs, New Jersey, Prentice-Hall.

Goodwin, R. (1980) 'Two decades of research into early language', in Sants, H.J. (ed.) *Developmental Psychology and Society*, London, Macmillan.

Kail, R.V. (1979) *The Development of Memory*, San Francisco, Freeman.

Pilling, D. and Kellmer-Pringle, M. (eds) (1978) *Controversial Issues in Child Development*, Part 5: 'Disadvantages and intervention', London, Paul Elek.

Slobin, D.I. (1979) *Psycholinguistics*, 2nd edn, Glenview, Illinois, Scott Foresman.

Chapter 4

Brown, A.L. and Campione, J.C. (1978) 'Memory strategies in learning: training children to study strategically', in Pick, H.L., Leibowitz, H.W., Singer, J.E. *et al.* (eds) *Psychology: From Research to Practice*, New York, Plenum.

Donaldson, M. (1978) *Children's Minds*, London, Fontana.

Floyd, A. (ed.) (1979) *Cognitive Development in the School Years*, London, Croom Helm.

Murray, F. V. (1981) 'The conservation paradigm: the conservation of conservation research', in Sigel, I.E., Brodzinsky, D.M. and Golinkoff, R.M. (eds) *New Directions in Piagetian Theory and Practice*, Hillsdale, New Jersey, Lawrence Erlbaum, 143–76.

Perret-Clermont, A.N. (1980) *Social Interaction and Cognitive Development in Children*, London, Academic Press.

Piaget, J. and Inhelder, B. (1969) *The Psychology of the Child*, London, Routledge & Kegan Paul.

Rosinski, R.R. (1977) *The Development of Visual Perception*, Santa Monica, California, Goodyear.

Chapter 5

Flavell, J.H. (1963) *The Developmental Psychology of Jean Piaget*, Princeton, New Jersey, Van Nostrand.

Keats, J.A., Collis, K.F. and Halford, G.S. (eds) (1978) *Cognitive Development. Research Based on a Neo-Piagetian Approach*, Chichester, West Sussex, Wiley.

Modgil, S. and Modgil, C. (1980) *Toward a Theory of Psychological Development*, Slough, NFER, Part VII.

Chapter 6

Denney, N.W. (1982) 'Ageing and cognitive change', in Wollman, B.B. (ed.) *Handbook of Developmental Psychology*, Englewood Cliffs, New Jersey, Prentice-Hall, pp. 807–27.

Kausler, D.H.L. (1982) *Experimental Psychology and Human Ageing*, Chichester, West Sussex, Wiley.

Maccoby, E.E. and Jacklin, C.N. (1974) *The Psychology of Sex Differences*, Stanford, California, Stanford University Press, part 1.

Salthouse, T.A. (1982) *Adult Cognition. An Experimental Psychology of Human Ageing*, New York, Springer.

Witkin, H.A. and Goodenough, D.R. (1981) *Cognitive Style: Essence and Origins. Field Dependence and Field Independence*, Psychological Issues, monograph, 51, New York, International Universities Press.

References and name index

The numbers in italics following each entry refer to page numbers in this book.

Altemeyer, R.A., Fulton, D. and Berney, K.M. (1969) 'Long-term memory improvement: confirmation of the finding by Piaget', *Child Development*, 40, 845–57. *53*

Anderson, J.R. and Bower, G.H. (1973) *Human Associative Memory*, Washington, DC, Winston Wiley. *51*

Appel, L.F., Cooper, R.G., McCarrell, N., Sims-Knight, J., Yussen, S.R. and Flavell, J.H. (1972) 'The development of the distinction between perceiving and memorising', *Child Development*, 43, 1365–81. *56*

Archer, J. and Lloyd, B. (1982) *Sex and Gender*, Harmondsworth, Middlesex, Penguin. *144, 145*

Arenberg, D.A. (1974) 'A longitudinal study of problem solving in adults', *Journal of Gerontology*, 29, 650–8. *139, 142*

Ariés, P. (1962) *Centuries of Childhood*, London, Cape. *75*

Aronson, E. and Rosenbloom, S. (1971) 'Space perception in early infancy: perception within a common auditory-visual space', *Science*, 172, 1161–3. *19*

Arvey, R.D. and Mussio, S.J. (1973) 'Test discrimination, job performance and age', *Industrial Gerontology*, 28, 22–9. *138*

Atkinson, R.C. and Shriffrin, R.M. (1968) 'Human memory: a proposed system and its control processes', in Spence, K.W. and Spence, J.T. (eds) *The Psychology of Learning and Motivation*, vol. 2, New York, Academic Press. *53*

Atwood, G. (1971) 'An experimental study of visual imagery and memory', *Cognitive Psychology*, 2, 290–9. *51*

Baddeley, A., Grant, S., Wight, E. and Thomson, N. (1975) 'Imagery and visual working memory', in Rabbitt, P.M.A. and Dornics, S. (eds) *Attention and Performance*, vol. 5, London, Academic Press. *51*

Ball, W. and Tronick, E. (1971) 'Infant response to impending collision: optical and real', *Science*, 171, 818–20. *18*

Bannister, D. and Mair, J.M.M. (1968) 'An evaluation of personal constructs', New York, Academic Press. *146*

Barrett, M.D. (1978) 'Ostensive definition and over-extension in child language', *Journal of Child Language*, 51, 205–19. *32*

Bartlett, F.C. (1932) *Remembering*, Cambridge, Cambridge University Press. *53*

Bates, E., Benigni, L., Brotherton, I., Camaioni, L. and Volterra, V. (1977) 'From gesture to the first word: on cognitive and social pre-requisites', in Lewis, M. and Rosenblum, L.A. (eds) *Interaction, Conversation and the Development of Language*, New York, Wiley. *35*

Bayley, N. (1933a) 'Mental growth during the first three years. A developmental study of sixty-one children by repeated tests', *Genetic Psychology Monographs*, 14, 1–92. *36*

Bayley, N. (1933b) *The California First-Year Mental Scale*, Berkeley, California, University of California Press. *36*

Bayley, N. (1935) *The Development of Motor Abilities during the First Three Years*, Monographs of the Society for Research in Child Development, 1. *36*

Bayley, N. (1940) 'Mental growth in young children', *Year book of the National Society for Studies in Education*, 39, 11–49. *42*

Bayraktar, R. (1979) 'Children's copying errors of simple geometric forms', unpublished D.Phil. thesis, University of Sussex, Brighton. *53*

Beilin, H. (1971) 'The development of physical concepts', in Mischel, T. (ed.) *Cognitive Development and Epistemology*, New York, Academic Press. *29*

Beilin, H. (1980) 'Piaget's theory: refinement, revision or rejection?' in Kluwe, R.H. and Spada, H. (eds) *Developmental Models of Thinking*, New York, Academic Press, 245–62. *10*

Bell, S. (1970) 'The development of the concept of object as related to infant mother attachment', *Child Development*, 41, 291–311. *28*

Beller, E.K. (1974) 'Impact of early education on disadvantaged children', in Ryan, S. (ed.) *A Report on Longitudinal Evaluations of Pre-School*

Programs, Washington, DC, Office of Child Development, Department of Health, Education and Welfare. *43*

Beller, E.K. (1979) 'Early intervention programmes', in Osofsky, J.D. (ed.) *Handbook of Infant Development*, New York, Wiley, 852–94. *42*

Belsky, J. and Steinberg, L.D. (1978) 'The effects of day care: a critical review', *Child Development*, 49, 929–49. *72*

Bennett, S.L. (1971) 'Infant-caretaker interactions', *Journal of the American Academy of Child Psychiatry*, 10, 321–35. *38*

Biggs, J.B. (1980), 'The relationship between developmental level and quality of school learning', in Modgil, S. and Modgil, C. (eds) *Toward a Theory of Psychological Development*, Slough, NFER, 591–634. *16*

Birns, B. (1965) 'Individual differences in human neonates' responses to stimulation', *Child Development*, 36, 249–56. *19, 37*

Block, J.H. (1979) 'Another look at sex differences in the socialisation behaviours of mothers and fathers', in Sherman, J. and Denmark, F. (eds) *Psychology of Women: Future Directions of Research*, New York, Psychological Dimensions, 25. *65*

Bloom, L. (1970) *Language Development: Form and Function in Emerging Grammars*, New York, Academic Press. *32, 60*

Blount, B.G. (1969) 'Acquisition of language by Luo children', working paper, no. 19, Language Behaviour Research Laboratory, University of California, Berkeley, California. *33*

Blum, J.E., Clark, E.T. and Jarvik, L.F. (1973) 'The New York State Psychiatric Institute study of aging twins', in Jarvik, L.F., Eisdorfer, C. and Blum, J.E. (eds) *Intellectual Functioning in Adults*, New York, Springer. *142*

Bower, T.G.R. (1977) *A Primer of Infant Development*, San Francisco, Freeman. *30*

Bower, T.G.R. (1979) *Human Development*, San Francisco, Freeman. *26*

Bower, T.G.R. (1982) *Development in Infancy*, 2nd edn, San Francisco, Freeman. *20, 26, 27*

Bower, T.G.R., Broughton, J.M. and Moore, M.K. (1970a) 'Infant response to approaching objects: an indicator of response to distal variables', *Perception and Psychophysics*, 9, 193–6. *18*

Bower, T.G.R., Broughton, J.M. and Moore, M.K. (1970b) 'Demonstration of intention in the reaching behaviour of neonate humans', *Nature*, 228, 679–81. *21*

Bowerman, M. (1973) 'Structural relationships in children's utterances, syntactic or semantic', in Moore, T.E. (ed.) *Cognitive Development and the Acquisition of Language*, New York, Academic Press. *34*

Braine, L.G. (1972) 'A developmental analysis of the effect of stimulus orientation on recognition', *American Journal of Psychology*, 85, 157–88. *59*

Braine, M.D.S. (1963) 'The ontogeny of English phrase structure: the first phase', *Language*, 39, 1–14. *95*

Brainerd, C.J. (1978) 'Learning research and Piagetian theory', in Siegel, L. and Brainerd, C.J. (eds) *Alternatives to Piaget: Critical Essays on the Theory*, New York, Academic Press, 69–110. *83*

Brimer, M.A. (1969) 'Sex differences in listening comprehension', *Journal of Research and Development in Education*, 3, 72–9. *144*

Bronfenbrenner, U. (1974) *Is Early Intervention Effective? A Report on Longitudinal Evaluation of Pre-School Programs*, Washington, DC, Office of Child Development, Department of Health, Education and Welfare. *72*

Brophy, J.E. (1970) 'Mothers as teachers of their own pre-school children: the influence of sociometric status and task structures on teaching specificity', *Child Development*, 41, 79–94. *65*

Brown, A.L. (1978) 'Knowing when, where and how to remember. A problem of meta-cognition', in Glaser, R. (ed.) *Advances in Instructional Psychology*, Hillsdale, New Jersey, Lawrence Erlbaum. *104*

Brown, A.L. and Scott, M.S. (1971) 'Recognition memory for pictures in pre-school children', *Journal of Experimental Child Psychology*, 11, 401–12. *55*

Brown, A.L. and Smiley, S.S. (1977) 'Rating the importance of structural units in prose passages. A problem of meta-cognitive development', *Child Development*, 48, 1–8. *103*

Brown, M. (1979) 'Cognitive development and the learning of mathematics', in Floyd, A. (ed.) *Cognitive Development in the School Years*, London, Croom Helm; Milton Keynes, Buckinghamshire, Open University Press, 351–73. *134*

Brown, R.E. (1973) *A First Language*, London, George Allen & Unwin. *34, 60, 61*

Brown, R.E. and Halpern, F. (1971) 'The variable pattern of rural black children', *Clinical Pediatrics*, 10. *42*

Bruner, J.S. (1966a) 'On the conservation of liquids', in Bruner, J.S., Olver, R.R., Greenfield, P.M. (eds) *Studies in Cognitive Growth*, New York, Wiley, 183–207. *92*

Bruner, J.S., *et al.* (1966b) 'On cognitive growth II', in Bruner, J.S., Olver, R.R. and Greenfield, P.M. (eds) *Studies in Cognitive Growth*, New York, Wiley. *62*

Bruner, J.S. (1973) *Beyond the Information Given*, London, George Allen & Unwin. *63*

Bruner, J.S. (1974) 'Nature and uses of immaturity', in Connolly, K. and Bruner, J. (eds) *The Growth of Competence*, London, Academic Press. *69*

Bruner, J.S. (1978) 'Learning how to do things with words', in Bruner, J. and Garton, A. (eds) *Human Growth and Development*, Milton Keynes, Buckinghamshire, Open University Press, 62–84. *34*

Bryant, P.E. (1972) 'Inferences in perception', paper presented to the British Psychological Society, London. *76*

Bryant, P.E. (1974) *Perception and Understanding in Young Children*, London, Methuen. *76, 93, 94*

Butterfield, E.C., Wambold, C. and Belmont, J.M. (1973) 'On the theory and practice of improving short-term memory', *American Journal of Mental Deficiency*, 77, 654–69. *13*

Carew, J.V. (1980) *Experience and the Development of Intelligence in Young Children at Home and in Day Care*, Monographs of the Society for Research in Child Development, 187. *40*

Carey, S. (1974) 'Cognitive competence', in Connolly, K. and Bruner, J. (eds) *The Growth of Competence*, London, Academic Press. *68*

Carey, S. and Diamond, R. (1977) 'From piecemeal to configurational representation of faces', *Science*, 195, 312–14. *55, 56*

Carpenter, G. (1975) 'Mother's face and the new born', in Lewin, R. (ed.) *Child Alive*, London, Temple Smith. *18*

Carter, A.L. (1974) *The Development of Communication in the Sensori-Motor Period: A Case Study*, unpublished doctoral dissertation, University of California, Berkeley, California. *41*

Case, R. (1978) 'Intellectual development from birth to adulthood: a neo-Piagetian interpretation', in Siegler, R.S. (ed.) *Children's Thinking. What Develops?*, Hillsdale, New Jersey, Lawrence Erlbaum, 37–72. *124*

Cattell, P. (1940) *The Measurement of Intelligence in Infants and Young Children*, Science Press, New York, reprinted 1960, Psychological Corporation. *36*

Chance, J., Overcast, T. and Dollinger, S.J. (1978) 'Ageing and cognitive regression: contrary findings', *Journal of Psychology*, 98, 177–83. *42*

Chandler, M. and Boyes, M. (1982) 'Social-cognitive development', in Wolman, B.B. and Stricker, G. (eds) *Handbook of Developmental Psychology*, Englewood Cliffs, New Jersey, Prentice-Hall, 387–402. *45, 46*

Charness, N. (1981a) 'Ageing and skilled problem solving', *Journal of Experimental Psychology: General*, 110, 21–38. *139*

Charness, N. (1981b) 'Search in Chess: age and skill differences', *Journal of Experimental Psychology: Human Perception and Performance*, 7, 467–76. *139*

Charness, N. (1981c) 'Visual short term memory and ageing in chess players', *Journal of Gerontology*, 36, 615–19. *139*

Chase, W.G. and Simon, H.A. (1973) 'The mind's eye in chess', in Chase, W.G. (ed.) *Visual Information Processing*, London, Academic Press. *97*

Chazan, M. (ed.) (1978) *International Research in Early Childhood Education*, Slough, NFER. *72*

Chi, M.T. (1976) 'Short term memory limitations in children. Capacity of processing deficits', *Memory and Cognition*, 4, 5, 559–72. *56*

Chi, M.T. (1977) 'Age differences in memory span', *Journal of Experimental Child Psychology*, 23, 266–81. *56*

Chi, M.T. (1978) 'Knowledge structures and memory development', in Siegler, R.S. (ed.) *Children's Thinking. What Develops?*, Hillsdale, New Jersey, Lawrence Erlbaum. *97*

Chomsky, N. (1965) *Aspects of the Theory of Syntax*, Cambridge, Massachusetts, MIT Press. *59*

Cicirelli, V.G. (1976) 'Categorisation behaviour in aged subjects', *Journal of Gerontology*, 31, 676–80. *138*

Clark, E.V. (1973) 'What's in a word? On the child's acquisition of semantics in his first language', in Moore, T.E. (ed.) *Cognitive Development and the Acquisition of Language*, New York, Academic Press. *32*

Clayton, V. and Overton, W.F. (1976) 'Concrete and formal operational thought processes in young adulthood and old age', *International Journal of Ageing and Human Development*, 7, 237–48. *138*

Cole, M. and Scribner, S. (1974) *Culture and Thought. A Psychological Introduction*, New York, Wiley. *113*

Collins, J.T. and Hagan, J.W. (1979) 'A constructivist account of the development of perception, attention, and memory', in Hall, G. and Lewis, M. (eds) *Attention and the Development of Cognitive Skills*, New York, Plenum. *57*

Collis, K.F. (1975) *A Study of Concrete and Formal Operations in School Mathematics: A Piagetian Viewpoint*, Melbourne, Victoria, Australian Council for Educational Research. *116*

Collis, K.F. (1976) 'Mathematical thinking in children', in Varma, V.P. and Williams, P. (eds) *Piaget, Psychology and Education*, London, Hodder & Stoughton, 144–54. *118, 133*

Collis, K.F. (1980) 'School mathematics and stages of development', in Modgil, S. and Modgil, C. (eds) *Toward a Theory of Psychological Development*, Slough, NFER, 635–71. *117*

Condon, W.S. and Sander, L. (1974) 'Neonate movement is synchronised with adult speech: interactional participation and language acquisition', *Science*, 183, 99–101. *19*

Cosgrove, J.M. and Patterson, C.J. (1977) 'Plans and the development of listener skills', *Developmental Psychology*, 13, 557–64. *103, 104*

Cromer, R.F. (1974) 'The development of language and cognition: the cognition hypothesis', in Foss, B. (ed.) *New Perspectives in Child Development*, Harmondsworth, Middlesex, Penguin. *60*

Dahlem, N.W. (1968) 'Reconstructive memory in kindergarten children', *Psychonomic Science*, 13, 331–2. *53*

Dahlem, N.W. (1969) 'Reconstructive memory in kindergarten children revisited', *Psychonomic Science*, 17, 101–3. *53*

Danner, F.W. (1976) 'Children's understanding of inter-sentence organisation in the recall of short descriptive passages', *Journal of Educational Psychology*, 68, 174–83. *103*

Dasen, P.R. (1977) (ed.) *Piagetian Psychology: Cross-cultural Contributions*, New York, Gardner Press. *128*

Dawes, R. (1975) 'The mind, the model and the task', in Restle, F., Shriffrin, R.M., Castellan, N.J., Lindman, H.R. and Pisoni, D.B. (eds) *Cognitive Theory*, vol. 1, 119–29, Hillsdale, New Jersey, Lawrence Erlbaum. *6*

Décarie, T.G. (1978) 'Affect development and cognition in a Piagetian context', in Lewis, M. and Rosenblum, L.A. (eds) *The Development of Affect*, New York, Plenum. *28*

De Groot, A. (1979) *Thought and Choice in Chess*, 2nd edn, The Hague, Mouton. *97*

De La Marre, G. and Shephard, R.D. (1958) 'Changes in speed and quality of work among leather cutters', *Occupational Psychology*, 32, 204–9. *138*

Demany, L., McKenzie, B. and Vurpillot, E. (1977) 'Rhythm perception in early infancy', *Nature*, 266, 718–19. *201*

Denney, N.W. (1974a) 'Classification criteria in middle and old age', *Developmental Psychology*, 10, 901–6. *138*

Denney, N.W. (1974b) 'Evidence for developmental change in categorisation criteria for children and adults', *Human Development*, 17, 41–53. *138*

Denney, N.W. (1982) 'Ageing and cognitive changes', in Wolman, B.B. (ed.) *Handbook of Developmental Psychology*, Englewood Cliffs, New Jersey, Prentice-Hall, 807–27. *138, 139, 140*

Denney, N.W., Jones, F.W. and Krigel, S.W. (1979) 'Modifying the questioning strategies of young children and elderly adults', *Human Development*, 22, 23–36. *139*

Denney, N.W. and Palmer, A.M. (1980) 'Adult age differences in traditional and practical problem-solving measures', unpublished manuscript, University of Kansas. *136, 139*

Denney, N.W. and Wright, J.C. (1978) 'Cognitive changes during the adult years. Implications for developmental theory and research', paper presented to the American Psychological Association, Toronto. *139*

Dennis, W. and Mallinger, B. (1949) 'Animism and related tendencies in senescence', *Journal of Gerontology*, 4, 218–21. *138*

De Silva, W.A. (1972) 'The formation of historical concepts through contextual cues', *Educational Review*, 24, 174–82. *118*

Dodd, B. (1972) 'Effects of social and vocal stimulation on infant babbling', *Developmental Psychology*, 7, 80–3. *31*

Donaldson, M. and Wales, R. (1970) 'On the acquisition of some relational terms', in Hayes, J.R. (ed.) *Cognition and the Development of Language*, New York, Wiley, 235–68. *87*

Doppelt, J.E. and Wallace, W.L. (1955) 'Standardisation of the Wechsler adult intelligence scale for older persons', *Journal of Abnormal and Social Psychology*, 51, 312–30. *136*

Dore, J. (1974) 'A pragmatic description of early language development', *Journal of Psycholinguistic Research*, 4. *29, 31*

Dore, J. (1975) 'Holophrases, speech acts and language universals', *Journal of Child Language*, 2, 21–39. *35*

Edwards, D. (1978) 'The sources of children's early meanings', in Markova, I. (ed.) *The Social Context of Language*, Chichester, Wiley. *32*

Eimas, P.D. (1975) 'Developmental studies of speech perception', in Cohen, L.B. and Salapatek, P. (eds) *Infant Perception: From Sensation to Cognition*, vol. 2, New York, Academic Press, 193–231. *20*

Eimas, P.D., Siqueland, E.R., Jusczyk, P. and Vigorito, J. (1971) 'Speech perception in infants', *Science*, 171, 303–6, reprinted in Stone, L.J., Smith, H.T. and Murphy, L.B. (eds) *The Competent Infant*, London, Tavistock, 1180–4. *19*

Elkind, D. (1970) 'Developmental studies in figurative perception', in Lipsitt, L.P. and Reese, H.W. (eds) *Advances in Child Behaviour and Development*, 4, 2–29. *96*

Ervin, S. (1964) 'Imitation and structural change in children's language', in Lenneberg, E.H. (ed.) *New Directions in the Study of Language*, Cambridge, Massachusetts, MIT Press. *34*

Ervin-Tripp, S.M. (1966) 'Language development', in Hoffman, L.W. and Hoffman, M.L. (eds) *Review of Child Development*, New York, Russell-Sage. *32*

Ervin-Tripp, S.M. (1973) 'Some strategies for the first two years', in Moore, T.E. (ed.) *Cognitive Development and the Acquisition of Language*, New York, Academic Press. *33*

Fagan, J.R. (1972) 'Infants' recognition memory for faces', *Journal of Experimental Child Psychology*, 14, 453–76. *96*

Fairweather, H. (1976) 'Sex differences in cognition', *Cognition*, 4, 231–80. *144*

Fantz, R.L. (1958) 'Pattern vision in young infants', *Psychological Research*, 8, 43–8. *17*

Fantz, R.L. (1966) 'Pattern discrimination and selective attention as determinants of perceptual development from birth', in Kidd, A.H. and Rivoire, J.L. (eds) *Perceptual Development in Children*, New York, International Universities Press. *17, 18*

Fantz, R.L., Ordy, J.M. and Udelf, M.S. (1962) 'Maturation of pattern vision in infants during the first six months', *Journal of Comparative and Physiological Psychology*, 55, 907–17. *17*

Faulkender, P.S., Wright, S.C. and Waldron, A. (1974) 'A generalized habituation of concept stimuli in toddlers', *Child Development*, 45, 1002–10. *55*

Fischer, K. W. (1980) 'A theory of cognitive development: the control and construction of hierarchies of skills', *Psychological Review*, 87, 6, 477–531. *10, 12, 112*

Flavell, J.H. (1963) *The Developmental Psychology of Jean Piaget*, Princeton, New Jersey, Van Nostrand. *108*

Flavell, J.H. (1970) 'Cognitive changes in adulthood', in Goulet, L.R. and Baltes, P.B. (eds) *Lifespan Developmental Psychology Research and Theory*, New York, Academic Press, 248–57. *135*

Flavell, J.H. (1971) 'First discussants' comments: what is memory development the development of?', *Human Development*, 14, 272–8. *53*

Flavell, J.H. (1976) 'Metacognitive aspects of problem solving', in Resnick, L.B. (ed.) *The Nature of Intelligence*, Hillsdale, New Jersey, Lawrence Erlbaum, p. 364. *12*

Flavell, J.H. (1977) *Cognitive Development*, Englewood Cliffs, New Jersey, Prentice-Hall. *98, 128*

Flavell, J.H. (1978) 'Metacognitive development', in Scandura, J.M. and Brainerd, C.J. (eds) *Structural Process Theories of Complex Human Behaviour*, Alphen a.d. Rijn, Netherlands, Sijthoff & Hoordhoff, p. 612. *12*

Flavell, J.H., Beach, D.H. and Chinsky, J.M. (1966) 'Spontaneous verbal rehearsal in a memory task as a function of age', *Child Development*, 37, 283–99. *56*

Flavell, J.H., Everett, B.A., Croft, K. and Flavell, E.R. (1981) 'Young children's knowledge about visual perception. Further evidence for the level 1–level 2 distinction', *Developmental Psychology*, 17, 1, 99–103. *46*

Flavell, J.H. and Wellman, H.M. (1977) 'Metamemory', in Kail, R.V. and Hagen, J.W. (eds) *Memory in Cognitive Development*, Hillsdale, New Jersey, Lawrence Erlbaum. *12, 48, 98*

Fluck, M. and Hewison, Y. (1979) 'The effect of televised presentation on number conservation in 5 year olds', *British Journal of Psychology*, 70, 507–9. *91*

Forrest, D.L. and Waller, T.G. (1979) *Cognitive and Metacognitive Aspects of Reading*, paper presented at the biennial meeting of the Society for Research in Child Development, San Francisco. *106*

Fraser, C., Bellugi, U. and Brown, R. (1963) 'Control of grammar in imitation, comprehension and production', *Journal of Verbal Learning and Verbal Behaviour*, 2, 121–35. *34*

Freedman, D.G. (1974) *Human Infancy: An Evolutionary Perspective*, Hillsdale, New Jersey, Lawrence Erlbaum. *29*

Freeman, N.H. and Janikoun, R. (1972) 'Intellectual realism in children's drawings of a familiar object with distinctive features', *Child Development*, 43, 1116–21. *50*

Furby, L. (1980) 'Implications of cross-cultural Piagetian research for cognitive developmental theory', in Modgil, S. and Modgil, C. (eds) *Toward a Theory of Psychological Development*, Slough, NFER, 541–6. *111*

Gardner, H. (1970) 'Children's sensitivity to painting styles', *Child Development*, 41, 813–21. *94*

Gardner, H. (1972a) 'The development of sensitivity to figural and stylistic aspects of paintings', *British Journal of Psychology*, 63, 605–15. *94*

Gardner, H. (1972b) 'Style sensitivity in children', *Human Development*, 15, 325–38. *94*

Garvey, C. and Hogan, R. (1973) 'Social speech and social interaction: egocentrism revisited', *Child Development*, 44, 562–8. *61*

Gersell, A. and Amatruda, C. (1941) *Developmental Diagnosis*, New York, Hoeber. *36*

Gibson, E.J. (1969) *Principles of Perceptual Learning and Development*, New York, Appleton-Century-Crofts. *96*

Gibson, E.J. (1970) 'The ontogeny of reading', *American Psychologist*, 25, 136–43. *97*

Ginsburg, H.P. (1981) 'Piaget and education: the contributions and limits of genetic epistemology', in Sigel, I.E., Brodzinsky, D.M. and Golinkoff, R.M. (eds) *New Directions in Piagetian Theory and Practice*, Hillsdale, New Jersey, Lawrence Erlbaum, 329–30. *115, 116*

Glachen, M. and Light, P. (1982) 'Peer interaction and learning: can two wrongs make a right?', in Butterworth, G. and Light, P. (eds) *Social Cognition*, Brighton, Harvester. *101*

Goldberg, S., Perlmutter, M. and Myers, N. (1974) 'Recall of related and unrelated lists by two year olds', *Journal of Experimental Child Psychology*, 18, 1–8. *21*

Golinkoff, R.A. (1976) 'A comparison of reading comprehension processes in good and poor comprehenders', *Reading Research Quarterly*, 11, 623–59. *103*

Gombrich, E.H. (1960) *Art and Illusion*, New York, The Bollinger Foundation. *50*

Gordon, I.J. and Guinagh, B.J. (1974) 'A home learning centre approach to early stimulation', final report of the National Institution of Mental Health project no. R01 MH 16037–01, University of Florida. *42*

Green, R.F. and Berkowitz, B. (1964) 'Changes in intellect with age. II: factorial analyses of Wechsler-Bellevue scores', *Journal of Genetic Psychology*, 104, 3–18. *139*

Greenfield, P.M. (1966) 'On culture and conservation', in Bruner, J.S.,

Olver, R.R. and Greenfield, P.M., *Studies in Cognitive Growth*, New York, Wiley. *112*

Griffiths, R. (1954) *The Abilities of Babies*, New York, McGraw-Hill. *36*

Grize, J.B. (1960) 'Du groupement au nombre: essai de formalisation', in Gréco, P., Grize, J.B., Papert, S. and Piaget, J., *Problèmes de la construction au nombre*, Études d'Épistémologie Génétique, vol. II, Paris, Presses Universitaires Françaises. *111*

Gruber, H.E. and Vonéche, J.J. (eds) (1977) *The Essential Piaget*, London, Routledge & Kegan Paul. *83*

Guinagh, B. J. and Gordon, I.J. (1976) *School Performance as a Function of Early Stimulation*, final report to Office of Child Development, Department of Health, Education and Welfare, Washington, DC. *42*

Hall, V.C. and Kaye, D.B. (1980) *Early Patterns of Cognitive Development*, Monographs of the Society for Research in Child Development, 184, 45, 2. *101, 102*

Hallam, R.N. (1970) 'Piaget and the teaching of history', *Educational Research*, 12, 3–12. *118*

Halliday, M.A.K. (1970) 'Language structure and language function', in Lyons, J. (ed.) *New Horizons in Linguistics*, Harmondsworth, Penguin, 140–65. *32*

Halliday, M.A.K. (1975a) 'Learning how to mean', in Lenneberg, E.H., (ed.) *Foundations of Language Development*, vol. I, New York, Academic Press; Paris, Unesco Press, 240–65. *33*

Halliday, M.A.K. (1975b) *Learning How to Mean*, London, Edward Arnold. *35*

Hallpike, C.R. (1976) 'Is there a primitive mentality?', *Man*, II, 253–70. *112*

Harvey, O.J., Hunt, D.E. and Schroder, H.M. (1961) *Conceptual Systems and Personality Organisation*, New York, Wiley. *146*

Heron, A. and Craik, F.I.M. (1964) 'Age differences in cumulative learning of meaningful and meaningless material', *Scandinavian Journal of Psychology*, 5, 209–17. *140*

Hertzig, M.E., Birch, H.G., Thomas, A. and Menduz, O.A. (1968) *Class and Ethnic Differences in the Responsiveness of Pre-school Children to Cognitive Demands*, Monographs of the Society for Research in Child Development, 117, 33, 1, Chicago, University of Chicago Press. *65, 66, 67*

Hess, R.D. and Shipman, V.C. (1965) 'Early experience and the socialisation of cognitive modes in children', *Child Development*, 36, 869–86. *64, 65*

Hess, R.D. and Shipman, V.C. (1967) 'Cognitive elements in maternal behaviour', in Hill, J.P. (ed.) *Minnesota Symposia on Child Psychology*, vol. I, Minneapolis, University of Minnesota Press. *64*

Hochberg, J. and Brooks, V. (1962) 'Pictorial recognition as an unlearned ability. A study of one child's performance', *American Journal of Psychology*, 75, 624–8. *96*

Home, H.J. (1966) 'The concept of mind', *International Journal of Psycho-Analysis*, 47, 42–9. *119*

Honzig, M.P., MacFarlane, J.W. and Allen, L. (1948) 'The stability of mental test performance between two and 18 years', *Journal of Experimental Education*, 4, 309–24. *42*

Hooper, F.H., Fitzgerald, J. and Papalia, D. (1971) 'Piagetian theory and the ageing process: extensions and speculations', *Ageing and Human Development*, 2, 3–20. *139*

Hull, L.C. (1943) *Principles of Behaviour*, New York, Appleton-Century-Crofts. *3*

Inhelder, B. (1962) 'Some aspects of Piaget's genetic approach to cognition', Monographs of the Society for Research in Child Development, 27, 2, 19–34. *9, 31*

Inhelder, B. and Piaget, J. (1955) *The Growth of Logical Thinking from Childhood to Adolescence*, London, Routledge & Kegan Paul. *121, 122, 123, 124*

Inhelder, B. and Piaget, J. (1959/1964) *The Early Growth of Logic in the Child*, London, Routledge & Kegan Paul. *80, 106, 107*

Istomina, Z.M. (1948/1974) 'The development of voluntary memory in pre-school age children', *Soviet Psychology*, 13, 5–64 (originally published in Russian). *57*

James, W. (1890) *The Principles of Psychology*, New York, Holt. *16*

Johnson-Laird, P.N., Legrenzi, P. and Sonino Legrenzi, M. (1972) 'Reasoning and a sense of reality', *British Journal of Psychology*, 63, 395–400. *126*

Jurd, M. (1978a) 'Concrete and formal operational thinking in history', in Keats, J.A., Collis, K.F. and Halford, G.S. (eds) *Cognitive Development. Research Based on a Neo-Piagetian Approach*, Chichester, Wiley, 285–314. *118, 134*

Jurd, M. (1978b) 'An empirical study of operational thinking in history type material', in Keats, J.A., Collis, K.F. and Halford, G.S. (eds) *Cognitive Development. Research Based on a Neo-Piagetian Approach*, Chichester, Wiley, 315–48. *118, 134, 137*

Kagan, J. (1979) *The Growth of the Child*, chap. 3: 'The growth of the infant's mind', London, Methuen, 62–73. *17*

Kagan, J., Klein, R.E., Finley, G.E., Rogoff, B. and Nolan, E. (1979) *A Cross-Cultural Study of Cognitive Development*, Monographs of the Society for Research in Child Development, 180, 44–5. *98, 99, 113*

Kail, R. and Hagen, J.W. (1982) 'Memory in childhood', in Wolman, B.B. and Stricker, G. (eds) *Handbook of Developmental Psychology*, Englewood Cliffs, New Jersey, Prentice-Hall. *53, 55*

Kamii, C. (1981) 'Application of Piaget's theory to education: the pre-operational level', in Sigel, I.E., Brodzinsky, D.M. and Golinkoff, R.M. (eds) *New Directions in Piagetian Theory and Practice*, Hillsdale, New Jersey, Lawrence Erlbaum, 231–66. *70, 71*

Kamii, C. and De Vries, R. (1976) *Piaget, Children and Number*, Washington, DC, National Association for the Education of Young Children. *69*

Kamii, C. and De Vries, R. (1977) 'Piaget for early education', in Day, M.C. and Parker, R.K. (eds) *The Pre-School in Action*, Boston, Allyn & Bacon. *70*

Karabenick, J.D. and Miller, S.A. (1977) 'The effects of age, sex and listener feedback on grade school children's referential communication', *Child Development*, 48, 678–83. *103*

Karmiloff-Smith, A. (1979) 'Micro and macro developmental changes in language acquisition and other representational systems', *Cognitive Science*, 3, 81–118. *78, 91*

Karplus, R. (1981) 'Education and formal thought. A modest proposal', in Sigel, I.E., Brodzinsky, D.M. and Golinkoff, R.M. (eds) *New Directions in Piagetian Theory and Practice*, Hillsdale, New Jersey, Lawrence Erlbaum, 285–314. *126, 129, 130, 131*

Kellogg, R. (1969) *Analysing Children's Art*, Palo Alto, California, National Press Books. *50*

Kelly, G.A. (1955) *The Psychology of Personal Constructs*, New York, Norton. *146*

Kendler, H.H. and Kendler, T.S. (1962) 'Vertical and horizontal processes in problem solving', *Psychological Review*, 69, 1–16. *4*

Kendler, H.H. and Kendler, T.S. (1971) 'Definitely our last word', *Psychological Bulletin*, 75, 290–3. *4*

Kendler, H.H. and Kendler, T.S. (1975) 'From discrimination learning to cognitive development: a neobehavioural odyssey', in Estes, W.K. (ed.) *Handbook of Learning and Cognitive Processes*, vol. 1., *Introduction to Concepts and Issues*, Hillsdale, New Jersey, Lawrence Erlbaum. *4, 5*

Kendler, H.H., Glasman, L.D. and Ward, J.W. (1972) 'Verbal-labelling and cue training in reversal shift behaviour', *Journal of Experimental Child Psychology*, 13, 195–209. *5*

Kendler, T.S., Kendler, H.H. and Learnard, B. (1962) 'Mediated responses to size and brightness as a function of age', *American Journal of Psychology*, 7, 571–86. *4*

Kendler, T.S. and Ward, J.W. (1972) 'Optional reversal probability as a linear function of the log of age', *Developmental Psychology*, 7, 337–48. *4*

Kepes, G. (1945) *The Language of Vision*, Chicago, Theobald. *96*

Kernan, K.T. (1969) 'The acquisition of language by Samoan children', unpublished doctoral dissertation, University of California, Berkeley, California. *33*

Klahr, D. (1980) 'Information processing models of intellectual development', in Klume, R.H. and Spada, H. (eds) *Developmental Models of Thinking*, New York, Academic Press, 127–62. *6*

Klahr, D. and Siegler, R.S. (1978) 'The representation of children's knowledge', in Reese, H.W. and Lippitt, L.L. (eds) *Advances in Child Development and Behaviour*, vol. 12, New York, Academic Press. *126*

Kohlberg, L. and Gilligan, C. (1971) 'The adolescent as philosopher. The discovery of the self in a post-conventional world', *Daedalus: Journal of the American Academy of Arts and Sciences*, vol. 100, no. 4, 1051–86. *125, 128*

Kuhn, D. (1981) 'The role of self-directed activity in cognitive development', in Sigel, I.E., Brodzinsky, D.M. and Golinkoff, R.M. (eds) *New Directions in Piagetian Theory and Practice*, Hillsdale, New Jersey, Lawrence Erlbaum, 353–8. *119*

Kuhn, D., Langer, J., Kohlberg, L. and Haan, N. (1977) 'The development of formal operations in logical and moral judgement', *Genetic Psychology Monographs*, 95, 97–188. *138*

Labouvie-Vief, G. and Schell, D.A. (1982) 'Learning and memory in later life', in Wolman, B.B. (ed.) *Handbook of Developmental Psychology*, Englewood Cliffs, New Jersey, Prentice-Hall, 828–46. *141*

Legrenzi, P. (1971) 'Discovery as a means to understanding', *Quarterly Journal of Experimental Psychology*, 23, 417–22. *126*

Lehman, H.C. (1953) *Age and Achievement*, Princeton, New Jersey, Princeton University Press. *136*

Lehman, H.C. (1954) 'Man's creative production rate at different ages and in different countries', *Scientific Monthly*, 78, 321–6. *136*

Lehman, H.C. (1958) 'The chemist's most creative years', *Science*, 127, 1213–22. *136*

Lehman, H.C. (1962) 'The creative production rates of present versus past generations of scientists', *Journal of Gerontology*, 17, 409–17. *136*

Lehman, H.C. (1965) 'The production of masters' works prior to age 30', *Gerontologist*, 5, 24–30. *136*

Lehman, H.C. (1966) 'The most creative years of engineers and other technologists', *Journal of Genetic Psychology*, 108, 263–77. *136*

Lenneberg, E.H. (1964) 'A biological perspective of language', in Lenneberg, E.H. (ed.) *New Directions in the Study of Language*, Cambridge, Massachusetts, MIT Press. *33*

Lenneberg, E.H. (1967) *Biological Foundations of Language*, New York, Wiley. *33*

Lewis, M. and McGurk, H. (1972) 'Evaluation of infant intelligence', *Science*, 178, 1174–7. *42*

Light, P.H. (1979) *The Development of Social Sensitivity*, Cambridge, Cambridge University Press. *46, 65*

Light, P.H., Buckingham, N. and Robbins, A.H. (1979) 'The conservation task as an interactional setting', *British Journal of Educational Psychology*, 49, 304–10. *77, 78, 90*

Lloyd, B.B. and Burgess, J.W. (1974) 'Social interaction and the development of cognitive skills in primary school children', unpublished final report to the Social Science Research Council. *99*

Lunzer, E. (1978) 'Formal reasoning: a re-appraisal', in Presseisen, B., Goldstein, D. and Appel, M.H. (eds) *Language and Operational Thought*, vol. 2: *Topics in Cognitive Development*, New York, Plenum. *125*

Luria, A.R. (1961) *The Role of Speech in the Regulation of Normal and Abnormal Behaviour*, London, Pergamon. *62*

Maccoby, E.E. (1966) 'Sex differences in intellectual functioning', in Maccoby, E.E. (ed.) *The Development of Sex Differences*, Stanford, California, Stanford University Press. *143*

Maccoby, E.E. and Jacklin, C.N. (1974) *The Psychology of Sex Differences*, Stanford, California, Stanford University Press. *144*

MacFarlane, J.A. (1975) 'Olefaction in the development of social preferences in the human neonate', in Ciba Foundation Symposium, 33, *Parent–Infant Interaction*, Amsterdam, Associated Scientific Publishers. *20*

McGarrigle, J. and Donaldson, M. (1974) 'Conservation accidents', *Cognition*, 3, 341–50. *77, 78, 89, 113*

MacNamara, J. (1972) 'Cognitive basis of language learning in infants', *Psychological Review*, 79, 1–13. *33*

McNeill, D. (1970a) *The Acquisition of Language: The Study of Developmental Psycholinguistics*, New York, Harper & Row. *33*

McNeill, D. (1970b) 'The development of language', in Mussen, P. (ed.) *Carmichael's Manual of Child Psychology*, vol. 1, New York, Wiley. *33*

Manniche, E. and Falk, G. (1957) 'Age and the Nobel Prize', *Behavioural Science*, 2, 301–7. *137*

Mason, J.S. (1974) 'Adolescent judgement as evidenced in response to poetry', *Education Review*, 26, 124–39. *118*

Masur, E.F., McIntyre, C.W. and Flavell, J.H. (1973) 'Developmental changes in apportionment of study time among items in a multi-trial free recall task', *Journal of Experimental Child Psychology*, 15, 237–46. *97, 98*

Matalon, B. (1962) 'Etude génétique de l'implication', in Beth, E.W. *et al.* 'Implication, formalisation et logique naturelle', *Etudes d'épistémologie génétique*, 16, 69–93, Paris, Presses Universitaires Françaises. *125*

Menyuk, P. and Bernholtz, N. (1969) 'Prosodic features and child's language production', *Research Laboratory of Electronics, Quarterly Progress Report*, 93. *31*

Miller, P.H. (1979) 'Stimulus dimensions, problem solving and Piaget', in

Hale, G. and Lewis, M. (eds) *Attention and the Development of Cognitive Skills*, New York, Plenum, 97–118. *94*

Miller, P.H. and Heldmeyer, K.H. (1975) 'Perceptual information in conservation: effects of screening', *Child Development*, 46, 588–92. *92, 93*

Miller, S. (1975) 'On the nature and functioning of spatial representations: experiments with blind and sighted subjects', paper presented at the international meeting of the Experimental Psychology Society, Cambridge. *52*

Miller, S. and Brownell, C. (1975) 'Peers, persuasion and Piaget: dyadic interaction between conservers and non-conservers', *Child Development*, 46, 992–7. *100*

Moely, B.E., Olson, F.A., Halwes, J.G. and Flavell, J.H. (1969) 'Production deficiency in young children's clustered recall', *Developmental Psychology*, 1, 26–34. *56*

Morse, P.A. and Snowdon, C.T. (1975) 'An investigation of categorical speech discrimination by rhesus monkeys', *Perception and Psychophysics*, 17, 9–16. *20*

Mugny, G. and Doise, W. (1978) 'Socio-cognitive conflict and structure of individual and collective performances', *European Journal of Social Psychology*, 8, 181–92. *100*

Murphy, L.B. and Moriarty, A.E. (1976) *Vulnerability, Coping and Growth*, New Haven, Connecticut, Yale University Press. *37*

Murphy, R.J.L. (1980) 'Sex differences in GCE examination results and entry statistics', paper presented at the Sex Differentiation and Schooling Conference, Cambridge, 2–5 Jan. *145*

Murray, F.B. (1980) 'The generation of educational practice from developmental theory', in Modgil, S. and Modgil, C. (eds) *Toward a Theory of Psychological Development*, Slough, NFER, 567–90. *120*

Murray, F.B. (1981) 'The conservation paradigm: the conservation of conservation research', in Sigel, I.E., Brodzinsky D.M. and Golinkoff, R.M. (eds) *New Directions in Piagetian Theory and Practice*, Hillsdale, New Jersey, Lawrence Erlbaum, 143–76. *88*

Murrell, K.F.H. and Humphries, S. (1978) 'Age, experience and short-term memory', in Gruneberg, M.M., Morris, P.E. and Sykes, R.N. (eds) *Practical Aspects of Memory*, London, Academic Press. *140*

Myers, N.A. and Perlmutter, M. (1978) 'Memory in the years from two to five', in Ornstein, P.A. (ed.) *Memory Development in Children*, Hillsdale, New Jersey, Lawrence Erlbaum, 191–218. *54*

Neimark, E.D. (1975) 'Intellectual development during adolescence', in Horowitz, F.D. (ed.) *Review of Child Development Research*, vol. 4, Chicago, University of Chicago Press. *125, 128*

Nelson, K. (1971) 'Memory development in children: evidence from non-verbal tasks', *Psychonomic Science*, 25, 346–8. *55*

Nelson, K. (1973) *Structure and Strategy in Learning to Talk*, Monographs of the Society for Research in Child Development, 38, 149. *32*

Newcombe, N.E., Rogoff, B. and Kagan, J. (1977) 'Developmental changes in recognition memory for pictures of objects', *Developmental Psychology*, 13, 337–41. *55*

Newell, A. and Simon, H.A. (1972) *Human Problem Solving*, Englewood Cliffs, New Jersey, Prentice-Hall. *5, 6*

Newson, J. and Newson, E. (1976) 'On the social origins of symbolic functioning', in Varma, P. and Williams, P. (eds) *Piaget, Psychology and Education*, London, Hodder & Stoughton, 84–96. *28*

Norman, D.A., Gentner, D.R. and Stevens, A.L. (1976) 'Comments on learning schemata and memory representation', in Klahr, D. (ed.) *Cognition and Instruction*, Hillsdale, New Jersey, Lawrence Erlbaum. *13*

Paivio, A. (1969) 'Mental imagery in associative learning and memory', *Psychological Review*, 76, 241–63. *51*

Papalia, D.E. (1972) 'The status of several conservation abilities across the life span', *Human Development*, 15, 229–43. *138, 139*

Papoušek, H. (1967) 'Experimental studies of appetitional behaviour in human new borns and infants', in Stevenson, H.W. *et al.* (eds) *Early Behaviour: Comparative and Developmental Approaches*, New York, Wiley. *38*

Papoušek, H. (1969) 'Individual variability in learned responses in human infants', in Robinson, R.J. (ed.) *Brain and Early Behaviour*, London, Academic Press. *38*

Papoušek, H. and Papoušek, M. (1975) 'Cognitive aspects of pre-verbal social interaction between human infants and adults', in Ciba Foundation Symposium, 33, *Parent–Infant Interaction*, Amsterdam, Associated Scientific Publishers. *38*

Paraskevopoulos, J. and Hunt, McV. (1971) 'Object construction and imitation under differing conditions of rearing', *Journal of Genetic Psychology*, 119, 301. *26*

Paris, S.G. and Lindauer, B.K. (1976) 'The role of inference in children's comprehension and memory for sentences', *Cognitive Psychology*, 8, 217–27. *98*

Parsons, C. (1960) 'Inhelder and Piaget's *The Growth of Logical Thinking*', *British Journal of Psychology*, 51, 78. *125*

Pascual-Leone, J.C. (1980) 'Constructive problems of constructive theories: the current relevance of Piaget's work and a critique of information-processing simulation psychology', in Klume, R.H. and Spada, H. (eds) *Developmental Models of Thinking*, New York, Academic Press, 263–96. *10*

Perlmutter, M. (1978) 'What is memory ageing the ageing of?' *Developmental Psychology*, 14, 330–45. *140*

Perret-Clermont, A.N. (1980) *Social Interaction and Cognitive Development in Children*, London, Academic Press. *100*

Phillips, D.C. (1978) 'The Piagetian child and the scientist: problems of assimilation and accommodation', *Educational Theory*, 28, 316. *119*

Piaget, J. (1923/1926) *The Language and Thought of the Child*, London, Routledge & Kegan Paul. *49, 61*

Piaget, J. (1924/1926) *Judgement and Reasoning in the Child*, London, Routledge & Kegan Paul. *9, 76, 99*

Piaget, J. (1926/1929) *The Child's Conception of the World*, London, Routledge & Kegan Paul. *118*

Piaget, J. (1932) *The Moral Judgement of the Child*, London, Routledge & Kegan Paul. *115*

Piaget, J. (1936a/1952) *The Origins of Intelligence in Children*, New York, International Universities Press. *22, 23*

Piaget, J. (1936b/1954) *The Construction of Reality in the Child*, New York, Basic Books. *22, 24*

Piaget, J. (1946/1951) *Play, Dreams and Imitation in Childhood*, London, Routledge & Kegan Paul. *49, 58*

Piaget, J. (1955/1958) *The Growth of Logical Thinking*, London, Routledge & Kegan Paul. *109*

Piaget, J. (1963/1969) 'Language and intellectual operations', in Furth, H.G. (ed.) *Piaget and Knowledge: Theoretical Foundations*, Englewood Cliffs, New Jersey, Prentice-Hall. *61*

Piaget, J. (1964/1980) *Six Psychological Studies*, Brighton, Harvester. *47, 76*

Piaget, J. (1968) *On the Development of Memory and Identity*, Heinz Werner Lecture Series, vol. II, Massachusetts, Clark University Press. *48*

Piaget, J. (1970a) 'Piaget's theory', in Mussen, P. (ed.) *Carmichael's Manual of Child Psychology*, vol. I, New York, Wiley, 103–32. *58, 115, 116*

Piaget, J. (1970b) *The Science of Education and the Psychology of the Child*, New York, Orion Press. *111*

Piaget, J. (1970c/1972) *The Principles of Genetic Epistemology*, London, Routledge & Kegan Paul. *115*

Piaget, J. (1972a) 'Intellectual evolution from adolescence', *Human Development*, 15, 1–12. *121, 129*

Piaget, J. (1972b/1974c) 'The necessity and significance of comparative research in genetic psychology', in Piaget, J., *The Child and Reality*, London, Frederick Muller, 143–62. *10*

Piaget, J. (1972c/1974) 'Perception learning and empiricism', in Piaget, J., *The Child and Reality*, London, Frederick Muller, 93–107. *10*

Piaget, J. (1974/1980) *Experiments in Contradiction*, Chicago, University of Chicago Press. *86*

Piaget, J. (1975/1977) *The Development of Thought: Equilibration of Cognitive Structures*, New York, Viking.

Piaget, J. and Inhelder, B. (1948/1956) *The Child's Conception of Space*, London, Routledge & Kegan Paul. *45*

Piaget, J. and Inhelder, B. (1963a/1969) 'Intellectual operations and their development', in Fraisse, P. and Piaget, J. (eds) *Experimental Psychology: Its Scope and Method*, vol. 7: *Intelligence*, Routledge & Kegan Paul, 144–205. *83, 106, 109*

Piaget, J. and Inhelder, B. (1963b/1969) 'Mental images', in Fraisse, P. and Piaget, J. (eds) *Experimental Psychology: Its Scope and Method*, vol. 7: *Intelligence*, London, Routledge & Kegan Paul, 85–143. *92*

Piaget, J. and Inhelder, B. (1966a) *The Mental Imagery of the Child*, London, Routledge & Kegan Paul. *49*

Piaget, J. and Inhelder, B. (1966b/1969) *The Psychology of the Child*, London, Routledge & Kegan Paul. *23, 48, 49*

Piaget, J. and Inhelder, B. (1968/1973) *Memory and Intelligence*, London, Routledge & Kegan Paul. *49, 52*

Piaget, J., Sinclair, H. and Vinh Bang (1968) *Épistémologie et psychologie de l'identité*, vol. 24: *Études d'épistémologie génétique*, Paris, Presse Universitaires de France. *48*

Piaget, J. and Szeminska, A. (1941/1952) *The Child's Conception of Number*, London, Routledge & Kegan Paul. *81, 82*

Pinard, A. (1981) *The Conservation of Conservation*, Chicago, University of Chicago Press. *83*

Powers, J.E. and Lis, D.J. (1977) 'Field dependence, independence and performance with the passive transformation', *Perceptual and Motor Skills*, 45, 759–65. *147*

Preston, M. and Yeni-Komshian, G. (1967) *Studies of Development of Stop Consonants in Children*, Hoskins Laboratories, SR-11. *30*

Radin, N. (1976) 'The role of the father in cognitive, academic and intellectual development', in Lamb, M.E. (ed.) *The Role of the Father in Child Development*, New York, Wiley. *65*

Redshaw, M. and Hughes, J. (1975) *Cognitive Development in Primate Infancy*, paper presented to the 137th annual meeting of the British Association for the Advancement of Science, University of Surrey. *35*

Reid, J. (1966) 'Learning to think about reading', *Educational Research*, 9, 56–62. *103*

Renner, J.W. and Stafford, D.G. (1976) 'Operational levels of secondary students', in Renner, J.W. *et al.*, *Research, Teaching and Learning with the Piaget Model*, Norman, Oklahoma, University of Oklahoma Press, 90–109. *125, 128*

Riley, D.A. (1968) *Discrimination Learning*, Boston, Allyn & Bacon. *3*

Rheingold, H.L., Gerwitz, J.L. and Ross, H.W. (1959) 'Social conditioning and vocalisations in the infant', *Journal of Comparative and Physiological Psychology*, 52, 68–78. *30*

Rhys, W.T. (1972) 'Geography and the adolescent', *Educational Review*,

24, 183–96, reprinted in Floyd, A. (ed.) *Cognitive Development in the School Years*, London, Croom Helm; Milton Keynes, Buckinghamshire, Open University Press, 249–61. *118, 135, 137*

Rose, S.A. and Blank, M. (1974) 'The potency of context in children's cognition: an illustration through conservation', *Child Development*, 45, 499–502. *89*

Rousseau, J. J. (1762/1911) *Emile*, London, Dent. *70, 75*

Rubin, K.H. (1974) 'The relationship between spatial and communicative egocentrism in children and young and old adults', *Journal of Genetic Psychology*, 125, 295–301. *138*

Rubin, K.H. (1976) 'Extinction of conservation. A life span investigation', *Developmental Psychology*, 12, 51–6. *138*

Rushton, J.P. and Wiener, J. (1975) 'Altruism and cognitive development in children', *British Journal of Social and Clinical Psychology*, 14, 341–9. *146*

Russell, J. (1979) 'Children deciding on correct answers; social influence under the microscope', paper presented to the Developmental Section of the British Psychological Society, Southampton. *101*

Salapatek, P. (1975) 'Pattern perception in early infancy', in Cohen, L.B. and Salapatek, P. (eds) *Infant Perception: From Sensation to Cognition*, vol. 1: *Basic Visual Processes*, New York, Academic Press, 133–248. *19*

Salthouse, T.A. (1974) 'Using selective interference to investigate spatial memory representations', *Memory and Cognition*, 2, 749–57. *51*

Salthouse, T.A. (1982) *Adult Cognition. An Experimental Psychology of Human Ageing*, New York, Springer. *139, 140, 142*

Sanders, S., Laurendean, M. and Bergeon, J. (1966) 'Ageing and the concept of space: the conservation of surfaces', *Journal of Gerontology*, 21, 281–5. *138*

Sasanuma, S. (1974) 'Kanji versus Kana processing alexia with transient agraphia', *Cortex*, 10, 89–97. *52*

Scarr-Salapatek, K.S. (1976) 'An evolutionary perspective on infant intelligence: species patterns and individual variations', in Lewis, M. (ed.) *Origins of Intelligence: Infancy and Early Childhood*, London, Wiley, 165–97. *29, 42*

Selzer, S.C. and Denney, N.W. (1980) 'Conservation abilities in middle-aged and elderly adults', *International Journal of Ageing and Human Development*, 11, 135–46. *139*

Shayer, M. (1980) 'Piaget and science education', in Modgil, S. and Modgil, C. (eds) *Toward a Theory of Psychological Development*, Slough, NFER, 699–731. *118, 128, 133, 145*

Shayer, M., Küchemann, D.E. and Wylam, H. (1976) 'The distribution of Piagetian stages of thinking in British middle and secondary school children', *British Journal of Educational Psychology*, 46 (2), 164–73. *118, 129*

Shayer, M. and Wylam, H. (1978) 'The distribution of Piagetian stages of thinking in British middle and secondary school children: 11–14 to 16 year olds and sex differentials', *British Journal of Educational Psychology*, 48, 1, 62–70. *129, 145*

Sheppard, J.L. (1978a) 'From intuitive thought to concrete operations', in Keats, J.A., Collis, K.F. and Halford, G.S. (eds) *Cognitive Development Research Based on a Neo-Piagetian Approach*, Chichester, Wiley, 27–46. *110*

Sheppard, J.L. (1978b) 'A structural analysis of concrete operations', in Keats, J.A., Collis, K.F. and Halford, G.S. (eds) *Cognitive Development Research Based on a Neo-Piagetian Approach*, Chichester, Wiley, 47–86. *110*

Sherman, J.A. (1978) *Sex-Related Cognitive Differences*, Springfield, Illinois, Charles C. Thomas. *144*

Siegler, I.C. (1975) 'The terminal drop hypothesis. Fact or Antifact?', *Experimental Ageing Research*, 1, 169–85. *142*

Slobin, D.I. (1970) 'Universals of grammatical development in children', in Flores D'Arcais, G.B. and Levelt, W.J.M. (eds) *Advances in Psycholinguistics*, Amsterdam, North Holland, 174–84. *33*

Slobin, D.I. (1971) 'Developmental psycholinguistics', in Dingwall, W.O. (ed.) *A Survey of Linguistic Science*, College Park, Maryland, William Orr Dingwall Linguistics Program, University of Maryland. *60*

Smith, C.S. (1970) 'An experimental approach to children's linguistic competence', in Hayes, J.R. (ed.) *Cognition and the Development of Language*, New York, Wiley. *34*

Snow, C.E. and Ferguson, C.A. (eds) (1977) *Talking to Children*, Cambridge, Cambridge University Press. *61*

Sokolov, A.N. (1972) *Inner Speech and Thought*, London, Plenum. *62*

Spence, K.W. (1936) 'The nature of discrimination learning in animals', *Psychological Review*, 43, 427–49. *3*

Staub, S. (1973) 'The effect of three types of relationships on young children's memory for pictorial stimulus pairs', unpublished doctoral dissertation, Graduate School of Education, Harvard University, Cambridge, Massachusetts. *55*

Stauffer, R.G. (1969) *Directing Reading Maturity as a Cognitive Process*, New York, Harper & Row. *104*

Steinschneider, A., Lipton, E.L. and Richmond, J.B. (1966) 'Auditory sensitivity in the infant: effect of intensity on cardiac and motor responsivity', *Child Development*, 37, 233–52, reprinted in Stone, L.J., Smith, H.T. and Murphy, L.B. (eds) (1974) *The Competent Infant*, London, Tavistock, 337–41. *19*

Stevenson, H. (1970) 'Learning in Children', in Mussen, P.H. (ed.) *Carmichael's Manual of Child Psychology*, vol. 1, New York, Wiley. *76*

Stevenson, H.W. (1982) 'Influences of schooling on cognitive development', in Wagner, D.A. and Stevenson, H.W. (eds) *Cultural Perspectives on Child Development*, San Francisco, Freeman, 208–24. *113*

Streeter, L. (1976) 'Language perception of 2-month-old infants shows effects of both innate mechanisms and experience', *Nature*, 259, 39–41. *20*

Thornton, S. (1982) 'Challenging "early competence": a process oriented analysis of children's classifying', *Cognitive Science*, 6, 77–100. *79*

Tighe, T.J. and Tighe, L. (1972) 'Stimulus control in children's learning', in Pick, A. (ed.) *Minnesota Symposium of Child Psychology*, vol. 6, Minneapolis, University of Minnesota Press. *77*

Tizard, J. (1978) 'Nursery needs and choices', in Bruner, J.S. and Garton, A. (eds) *Human Growth and Development*, Milton Keynes, Buckinghamshire, Open University Press. *72*

Tonkova-Yampol'skaya (1968) 'Development of speech intonation in infants during the first two years of life', reprinted in Ferguson, C.A. and Slobin, D.I. (eds) (1973) *Studies of Child Language Development*, New York, Holt, Rinehart & Winston. *31*

Trevarthen, C. (1975) 'Early attempts at speech', in Lewin, R. (ed.) *Child Alive*, London, Temple Smith, 62–80. *30*

Trevarthen, C. (1977) 'Descriptive analysis of infant communicative behaviour', in Schaffer, H.R. (ed.) *Studies in Mother–Infant Interaction*, London, Academic Press, 227–70. *30*

Trevarthen, C. (1979a) 'The tasks of consciousness: how could the brain do them?', *Brain and Mind*, Ciba Foundation Series 69, Excerpta Medica, Elsevier North-Holland. *27*

Trevarthen, C. (1979b) 'Communication and co-operation in early infancy: a description of primary intersubjectivity', in Bullowa, M. (ed.) *Before Speech*, Cambridge, Cambridge University Press, 321–47. *16, 27, 30*

Trevarthen, C. (1982) 'The primary motives for co-operative understanding', in Butterworth, G. and Light, P. (eds) *Social Cognition*, Brighton, Harvester. *28*

Tucker, N. (1977) *What is a Child?*, London, Fontana. *75*

Tulving, E. (1972) 'Episodic and semantic memory', in Tulving, E. and Donaldson, W. (eds) *The Organization of Memory*, New York, Academic Press. *5*

Turner, J. (1980) *Made for Life*, London, Methuen. *38, 75*

Uzgiris, I.C. and Hunt, J. McV. (1966) 'An instrument for assessing infant psychological development', Psychological Development Laboratories, University of Illinois. *36*

Vacc, N.A. and Vacc, N.E. (1973) 'An adaptation for children of the Modified Role Reportory Test – a measure of cognitive complexity', *Psychological Reports*, 33, 771–6. *146*

Vuyk, R. (1981) *Overview and Critique of Piaget's Genetic Epistemology*, 1965–80, 2 vols, London, Academic Press. *80*

Vygotsky, L.S. (1962) *Thought and Language*, Cambridge, Massachusetts, MIT Press. *32, 58, 60*

Wagner, P.A. (1973) 'Memories of Morocco: the influence of age, schooling and environment on memory', *Cognitive Psychology*, 10, 1–28. *98*

Warren, N. (1980) 'Universality and plasticity, ontogeny and phylogeny: the resonance between culture and cognitive development', in Sants, J. (ed.) *Developmental Psychology and Society*, London, Macmillan, 290–326. *114*

Wason, P.C. and Johnson-Laird, P.N. (1972) *Psychology of Reasoning: Structure and Content*, London, Batsford. *125*

Wason, P.C. and Shapiro, D. (1971) 'Natural and contrived experiences in a reasoning problem', *Quarterly Journal of Experimental Psychology*, 23, 63–71. *126*

Waters, R.S. and Wilson Jr, W.A. (1976) 'Speech perception by rhesus monkeys: the voice distinction in synthesised labial and velar stop consonants', *Perception and Psychophysics*, 19, 299–309. *20*

Watson, J.B. (1913) 'Psychology as the behaviourists view it', *Psychological Review*, 20, 158–77. *3*

Weikart, D.P., Rogers, L., Adcock, C. and McClelland, O. (1971) *The Cognitively Oriented Curriculum*, Washington, DC, ERIC-NAEYC. *69*

Wellman, H.M. (1977) 'Preschoolers' understanding of memory relevant variables', *Child Development*, 48, 1720–3. *57*

Wellman, H.M., Ritter, K. and Flavell, J.H. (1975) 'Deliberate memory behaviour in the delayed reactions of very young children', *Developmental Psychology*, 11, 780–7. *57*

Wertheimer, M. (1961) 'Psycho-motor co-ordination of auditory-visual space at birth', *Science*, 134, 1692. *19*

Wheldall, K. and Poborca, B. (1980) 'Conservation without conversation? An alternative, non-verbal paradigm for assessing conservation of liquid quantity', *British Journal of Psychology*, 71, 117–34. *87*

White, B.L., Kaban, B.T. and Attanucci, J.S. (1979) *The Origins of Human Competence*, final report of the Harvard Pre-school Project, Lexington, Massachusetts, Lexington Books. *40, 41, 42, 43*

White, S.H. (1965) 'Evidence for a hierarchical arrangement of learning processes', *Advances in Child Development and Behaviour*, 2, 187–220. *75*

White, S. (1970) 'Learning theory function and child psychology', in Mussen, P.H. (ed.) *Carmichael's Manual of Child Psychology*, vol. 1, New York, Wiley. *76*

Witkin, H.A., Dyk, R.B., Paterson, H.F., Goodenough, D.R. and

Karp, S.A. (1962) *Psychological Differentiation*, New York, Wiley. *144, 147*

Witkin, H.A. and Goodenough, D.R. (1981) *Cognitive Style: Essence and Origins. Field Dependence and Field Independence*, New York, International Universities Press. *147, 148*

Witz, K.G. (1969) 'On the structure of Piaget's grouping I', *Archives de Psychologie*, 159, 37–49. *III*

Wolff, P. (1959) 'State and neonatal activity', *Psychosomatic Medicine*, 21, 110–18, reprinted in Stone, L.J., Smith, H.T. and Murphy, L.B. (eds) (1974) *The Competent Infant*, London, Tavistock, 257–68. *17*

Yarrow, L.J., Rubenstein, J.L. and Pedersen, F.A. (1975) *Infant and Environment*, Washington, DC, Hemisphere. *38, 39*

Younas, A. (1973) 'The development of spatial reference systems in the perception of shading information for depth', paper read to the Society for Research in Child Development, Philadelphia, Pennsylvania. *96*

Subject index

The reference section of this book serves as a name index. Names are included in this index only where there is no corresponding literature citation.